the food of
FRANCE

the food of
FRANCE

a journey for food lovers

Photography by Chris L. Jones
Recipes by Maria Villegas and
Sarah Randell

bay books

CONTENTS

FOOD JOURNEYS IN FRANCE

the food of
FRANCE

THE FRENCH PRESIDE OVER ONE OF THE WORLD'S GREAT CULINARY HERITAGES, FROM RIPE CAMEMBERT TO WARM CROISSANTS, EXQUISITE PÂTISSERIE AND VINTAGE CHAMPAGNE, AND NOWHERE IS IT BETTER, OR ENJOYED MORE, THAN IN FRANCE ITSELF.

France's reputation for wonderful food and cooking is often thought of as being based on technical skills and extravagant, expensive ingredients—on sauces that need to be reduced, and foie gras, truffles and other delicacies. This is *haute cuisine,* 'classic cooking', which was developed by the chefs of the French aristocracy and reached its heyday in the nineteenth century under legendary French chefs like Auguste Escoffier. *Haute cuisine* is a time-consuming artform that adheres to strict rules, and this elegant form of cooking requires an understanding of its special methods and techniques, skills honed by long apprenticeships in the kitchens of great restaurants, particularly in creating the subtle sauces that are its foundation. Nowadays this style of cooking is found mostly in expensive restaurants, but it can represent the highest art of cooking, one celebrated in stars by the famous Michelin guide.

Nouvelle cuisine, 'new cooking', was a reaction to the dominance of *haute cuisine* in the 1960s, when chefs, including Paul Bocuse and the Troisgros brothers, banded together to create lighter dishes, with less reliance on heavy sauces and a willingness to experiment with untraditional ingredients and cooking styles. *Nouvelle cuisine* encouraged innovation, and though some of its precepts were later abandoned, it had a lasting influence on French cooking.

Fundamentally, however, French food is a regionally based cuisine and many French dishes are called after their place of origin, from *entrecôte à la bordelaise, sole à la normande* to *boeuf à la bourguignonne.* Eating your way around France the

France is a strong agricultural nation and grows wonderful local produce, from French beans to cherries, apricots and redcurrants. They are sold in daily and weekly markets all over France, such as this one closing up after a busy morning in Périgueux. The land also supports a good dairy industry, with much milk used in cheeses. Cafés, like this Marseilles one, are a French institution.

Every town in France has a market selling local, seasonal produce such as these asparagus and eggs, and artisan-made bread, cheese and wines. On this page, bread is sold at a Provence market and vegetables and potatoes in a Paris market. Honfleur is one of France's many fishing ports. Wonderful pâtisserie *(opposite)* in Gérard Mulot's shop in Paris, and a typical French *petit déjeuner*.

PETRI ET FAÇONNE À LA MAIN

La Pièce

10F

regional differences are still very distinct, and most restaurants cook not only the local dishes, but those of their own town or village. This is a result not only of tradition, but also of an enduring respect for local produce, the *produits du terroir*. Each area of France grows or produces food uniquely suited to its terrain and climate, from Bresse chickens to walnuts from Grenoble, butter from Normandy and mustard from Dijon. Nowadays, there is more crossover between the provinces, and in markets, the best, not just the local, vegetables can be found, but the notion of regional specialities still underlies French cooking.

This respect for ingredients extends also to only eating fruit and vegetables at the height of their season. Recipes change to reflect the best that each month has to offer, and every month, seasonal fruits and vegetables are eagerly awaited, from the summer melons of Provence to autumn walnuts and winter truffles in the Dordogne.

The French have also gone to great lengths to protect their ingredients and traditional methods of food preparation. The strict *appellation d'origine contrôlée* (AOC) system that they use to keep their cheese and wines as authentic as possible, is also being extended to an increasing number of other important and regionally based food products, from Puy lentils to carrots from Créances.

The French love food and though many traditions have changed, and an office worker is just as likely to grab a quick sandwich on the run as enjoy a four-course lunch, as a foundation of French culture, eating and drinking remain incredibly important. One of the great joys of France is starting the morning with a *petit déjeuner* of a fresh croissant and a *café au lait*. Lunch is still for many the main meal of the day, though dinner may be equally substantial, and with many shops and work places closed between 12:30 and 3:30, it can extend to three or four courses with wine.

Despite the emergence of the *hypermarché,* specialist food shops and weekly markets are integral to the French way of life. There is a *boulangerie* in every village; meat is purchased at a *boucherie*; while a *charcuterie* specializes in pork products and delicatessen items and a *pâtisserie* in baked goods. Markets are usually held weekly, and in some areas you can follow the same stallholders from town to town through the week. Even Paris has its neighbourhood markets, and there are also speciality markets, such as the garlic market in Aix-en-Provence in July and the foie gras market in the winter in Sarlat in Périgord.

THE FOOD OF THE NORTH

Paris is a world culinary centre, where neighbourhood markets sell fantastic produce from all over France. Much of the city's reputation lies with its restaurants, a legacy of the revolution when private chefs had to find a new living. Parisians are legendarily discerning about their food and it is here you find the real home of the baguette, the country's most refined pâtisserie and finest cheese shops.

Brittany is traditionally a fishing and farming region with outstanding seafood, including native oysters, and wonderful early fruits and vegetables. Sweet crêpes and savoury buckwheat galettes are found throughout the region. Its sea salt, *sel de guerande*, is used all over France.

Normandy's rich pasture is home to some of France's greatest cheeses: Camembert, Pont l'Evêque and Livarot; along with crème fraîche, butter and apples—three classic ingredients in French cuisine. There is also pré-salé lamb (lamb raised in salt marshes), mussels, oysters, cider and calvados.

Known as 'the Garden of France', the Loire Valley produces fruit, vegetables and white wines. Wild mushrooms are grown in the caves of Saumur and regional dishes include rillettes, andouillettes and tarte Tatin. The region also produces fine goat's cheeses, including Crottin de Chavignol. Poitou-Charentes on the Atlantic Coast has some of France's best oyster beds near Marennes, and is home to Charentais melons, unsalted butter and Cognac.

Nord-Pas-de-Calais along the coast includes Boulogne-sur-mer, France's biggest fishing port. Inland are found the washed-rind Maroilles cheese, andouillettes and Flemish beers, used for cooking in dishes such as *carbonnade à la flamande*. Picardie has vegetables, fruit and pré-salé lamb.

Champagne-Ardennes is a rural region, with Champagne famous not just for its wine, but also for cheeses such as Brie and Chaource. In the rugged north, the game forests of Ardennes have created a tradition of charcuterie. Jambon d'Ardennes and pâtés d'Ardennes are world-famous.

Bordering Germany, Alsace-Lorraine's mixed heritage is reflected in its cuisine. Its charcuterie is used in quiche lorraine, *choucroute garnie*, *tarte flambée* and *baeckenoffe* (stew). Meat dishes *à la lorraine* are served with red cabbage cooked in wine, while Alsace's baking has Germanic influences, with pretzels, rye bread and kugelhopf.

Paris has a wonderful choice of food with the finest produce brought to the capital from all over France. It is known for its baguettes, upmarket *traiteurs* (take-out food shops) and pavement cafés. Cabbage is used in many local Alsace-Lorraine dishes, while oysters, apples and soft cheeses are eaten all over Normandy and Brittany, such as in these waterfront cafés in Honfleur.

11

Lyon's Quai Saint Antoine market in this gastronomic city sells everything from eggs and spring onions (scallions) to potatoes and charcuterie. Limousin is a meat-rearing area and home to wild mushrooms. Mild red onions grow in Burgundy, pears are a Savoie speciality and chickens from Bresse have AOC status. Cheeses from the Alps are among France's best.

THE FOOD OF THE EAST AND CENTRE

Central France is made up of the regions of Auvergne and Limousin. With very cold winters, the cuisine of these areas tends to be hearty and potatoes and cabbages are heavily used for dishes such as *aligot* and *potée auvergnate* (one-pot pork and cabbage stew). Limousin is famous for its beef, lamb, pork and veal and Auvergne for its game and tiny green Puy lentils. The area also produces Cantal and Saint Nectaire cheeses, as well as blue cheeses such as Bleu d'Auvergne and Fourme d'Ambert. Auvergne is known for its bottled mineral waters, including Vichy and Volvic.

Burgundy is world-famous for its red and white wines with the wine industry centred around the town of Beaune. Burgundian dishes tend to be rich, full of flavour and a perfect match for the area's wines. Wine is also an important part of the region's cooking, and *à la bourguignonne* usually means cooked in red wine. Boeuf bourguignon, coq au vin, Bresse chicken cooked with cream and wild morels, snails filled with garlic herb butter and slices of *jambon persillé* (ham and parsley set in aspic) are all Burgundian classics. Dijon is synonymous with mustard and is also the home of *pain d'épices* (spicy gingerbread) and kir, made of white wine and *crème de cassis* from local blackcurrants.

One of France's great gastronomic capitals, Lyon is home to great restaurants, including Paul Bocuse's, as well as many simple *bouchons* (traditionally working-class cafés) and brasseries all over the city. Considered to be the charcuterie centre of France, Lyon is renowned for its andouillettes, cervelas and rosette sausages, served at *bouchons* along with *salade lyonnaise*, pike quenelles, *poulet au vinaigre* (chicken stewed in vinegar), potato gratins, the fresh herb cheese, *cervelle de canut* (silk-weavers' brains) and *pots* (one pint bottles) of local Beaujolais or Côtes du Rhône. The surrounding countryside produces excellent fruit and vegetables, as well as AOC chickens from Bourg-en-Bresse.

The East of France rises up into the French Alps and is made up of three regions, Franche-Comté in the north and Savoie and Dauphiné in the south. These mountain regions have great cheesemaking traditions and in the summer, *alpages* cheeses such as Reblochon are still made from animals taken up to the high meadows. Tomme de Savoie, Beaufort and Comté are other mountain cheeses and dishes include fondues and raclettes. Potatoes are found all over the Centre and East, but it is Dauphiné that gives its name to the famous *gratin dauphinois*.

THE FOOD OF THE SOUTH AND SOUTHWEST

Bordeaux is associated with great wines and the *grands crus* of Médoc and Saint Emilion are world-famous, as are dessert wines from Sauternes. Red wine is used in cooking and these dishes are usually known as *à la bordelaise*, such as *entrecôte à la bordelaise*. Oysters from the Atlantic beds at Arcachon and pré-salé lamb from Pauillac are specialities.

Goose and duck confit and foie gras are the Dordogne and Lot's most famous exports along with the black truffles and walnuts of Périgord. Black truffles and foie gras are used as a garnish in many southwest dishes and these dishes are sometimes known as *à la périgourdine*. Walnuts are used in *salade aux noix* and in oils, and prunes are grown at Agen.

Gascony is a largely rural area that produces Armagnac and is famous, along with the Dordogne, for its foie gras, duck and goose confit, pâtés and terrines and for the use of goose fat in its cooking. Home-made and local specialities can be tasted at *fermes auberges* (farmhouse restaurants).

The southwest Basque country close to Spain flavours its food with spicy *piment d'Espelette*, dried chillies, which are also often used in the salting mixture for the local Bayonne ham. Tuna are caught off the Atlantic coast and the tradition of baking, such as making *gâteau basque*, is strong.

The flavours of Provence are those of the Mediterranean: olives, olive oil, garlic, eggplants (aubergines), zucchini (courgettes), tomatoes and *herbes de provence,* along with melons from Cavaillon, strawberries and peaches. Provençal cuisine includes the strong flavours of aïoli, anchoïade and tapénade; pissaladière and pistou from the Italian-bordering Côte d' Azur; simple grilled fish and the classic bouillabaisse; red rice from the Camargue and honey and candied fruit.

Close to Spain, Languedoc-Roussillon is home to the famous Roquefort blue cheese, which is aged in caves. Along the coast, anchovies are conserved and the area uses salt cod in dishes such as *brandade de morue*. There is fresh seafood from the Mediterranean and *bourride* is Languedoc's bouillabaisse. Inland, there is hearty cassoulet from Carcassonne, Castelnaudary and Toulouse, sausages from Toulouse and pink garlic from Tarn.

Corsica, closer to Italy and Sardinia than France, has a tradition of Italian charcuterie, pasta and polenta. *Stufato* is a classic rich beef stew, where the sauce is served over pasta.

Many great wines have been aged in Bordeaux's cellars, such as this one at Château Lafite-Rothschild. Tapénade, olives and garlic are the tastes of the South, while figs, lemons and tomatoes grow well in the hot climate. In Marseilles, tiny snails are sold alongside fish on the harbourfront. Black truffles are a winter speciality in the Dordogne and fougasse is a bread from Provence.

15

SOUPS

FRENCH ONION SOUP

THE ORIGINS OF THIS ONION SOUP ARE UNCLEAR, SOME CLAIMING IT TO BE A LYONNAIS INVENTION AND OTHERS CREDITING IT TO PARIS. THERE IS ALSO MUCH DISPUTE OVER HOW THE DISH SHOULD BE MADE: WHEN TO ADD THE BREAD AND WHETHER THE ONIONS ARE COARSELY SLICED OR PURÉED?

Lyon is certainly the area of France most associated with the onion: 'à la lyonnaise' means a dish containing onions.

50 g (1³/₄ oz) butter
750 g (1 lb 10 oz) onions, finely sliced
2 garlic cloves, finely chopped
40 g (¹/₃ cup) plain (all-purpose) flour
2 litres (8 cups) beef or chicken stock
250 ml (1 cup) white wine
1 bay leaf
2 sprigs of thyme
12 slices stale baguette
100 g (³/₄ cup) finely grated Gruyère

SERVES 6

MELT the butter in a heavy-based saucepan and add the onion. Cook over low heat, stirring occasionally, for 25 minutes, or until the onion is deep golden brown and beginning to caramelize.

ADD the garlic and flour and stir continuously for 2 minutes. Gradually blend in the stock and the wine, stirring all the time, and bring to the boil. Add the bay leaf and thyme and season. Cover the pan and simmer for 25 minutes. Remove the bay leaf and thyme and check the seasoning. Preheat the grill (broiler).

TOAST the baguette slices, then divide among six warmed soup bowls and ladle the soup over the top. Sprinkle with the grated cheese and grill (broil) until the cheese melts and turns light golden brown. Serve immediately.

CAULIFLOWER SOUP

30 g (1 oz) butter
1 onion, finely chopped
¹/₂ celery stalk, finely chopped
600 g (1 lb 5 oz) cauliflower, broken into florets
440 ml (1³/₄ cups) chicken stock
315 ml (1¹/₄ cups) milk
1 bay leaf
1 sprig of thyme
125 ml (¹/₂ cup) cream
freshly grated nutmeg
2 tablespoons chopped chives

SERVES 4

MELT the butter in a large saucepan and add the onion and celery. Cook over low heat until the vegetables are softened but not browned. Add the cauliflower, stock, milk, bay leaf and thyme and bring to the boil. Cover the pan, reduce the heat and simmer for 20 minutes, or until the cauliflower is tender.

LEAVE the soup to cool, then remove the bay leaf and thyme. Purée the soup until smooth in a blender or food processor and return to the clean saucepan. Bring to the boil, stirring constantly, add the cream and reheat without boiling. Season with salt, white pepper and nutmeg. Serve garnished with chives.

CAULIFLOWER SOUP

CHICKEN CONSOMMÉ

STOCK
1 kg (2 lb 4 oz) chicken carcasses,
  halved
200 g (7 oz) chicken legs
1 carrot, chopped
1 onion, chopped
1 celery stalk, chopped
2 sprigs of parsley
20 black peppercorns
1 bay leaf
1 sprig of thyme

CLARIFICATION MIXTURE
2 chicken legs
1 carrot, finely chopped
1 leek, finely chopped
1 celery stalk, finely chopped
10 black peppercorns
1 sprig of parsley, chopped
2 tomatoes, chopped
2 egg whites, lightly beaten

sea salt
1 small carrot, julienned
1/2 small leek, white part only,
  julienned

SERVES 4

TO MAKE the stock, remove any skin and fat from the chicken carcasses and legs and place in a large heavy-based saucepan with 3 litres (12 cups) cold water. Bring to the boil and skim any fat that floats to the surface. Add the remaining ingredients and simmer for 1 1/2 hours, skimming occasionally. Strain the stock (you should have about 1.5 litres/ 6 cups) and return to the clean saucepan.

TO MAKE the clarification mixture, remove the skin and meat from the chicken legs and discard the skin. Chop the meat finely (you will need about 150 g/5 1/2 oz) and mix with the carrot, leek, celery, peppercorns, parsley, tomato and egg white. Add 185 ml (3/4 cup) of the warm stock to loosen the mixture.

ADD the clarification mixture to the strained stock and whisk in well. Bring to a gentle simmer. As the mixture simmers the clarification ingredients will bind with any impurities and form a 'raft'. As the raft rises, gently move it with a wooden spoon to one side of the saucepan away from the main movement of the simmering stock (this will make it easier to ladle out the stock later). Simmer for 1 hour, or until the stock is clear.

LADLE OUT the chicken stock, taking care not to disturb the raft, and strain through a fine sieve lined with damp muslin. Place sheets of paper towel over the top of the consommé and then quickly lift away to remove any remaining fat. Season with coarse sea salt (or use other iodine-free salt, as iodine will cloud the soup).

JUST BEFORE serving, reheat the consommé. Put the julienned vegetables in a saucepan of boiling water and cook for 2 minutes until just tender. Drain well, spoon into warmed soup bowls and pour the consommé over the top.

Clarity is the hallmark of a good consommé. This soup uses a clarification mixture that forms a 'raft', to which all the impurities cling. The stock is then strained through fine muslin, leaving a beautifully transparent liquid.

CRAB BISQUE

ORIGINALLY BISQUES WERE MADE WITH POULTRY AND GAME BIRDS (IN PARTICULAR PIGEONS) AND WERE MORE OF A STEW. TODAY THEY HAVE EVOLVED INTO RICH VELVETY SOUPS AND TEND TO USE CRUSTACEANS. YOU CAN RESERVE SOME OF THE CRAB MEAT OR CLAWS FOR A GARNISH.

You will need a large saucepan or stockpot for making crab bisque—the crab shells take up a lot of room in the pan.

1 kg (2 lb 4 oz) live crabs
50 g (1³/₄ oz) butter
¹/₂ carrot, finely chopped
¹/₂ onion, finely chopped
1 celery stalk, finely chopped
1 bay leaf
2 sprigs of thyme
2 tablespoons tomato paste (purée)
2 tablespoons brandy
150 ml (5 fl oz) dry white wine
1 litre (4 cups) fish stock
60 g (2¹/₄ oz) rice
60 ml (¹/₄ cup) thick (double/heavy) cream
¹/₄ teaspoon cayenne pepper

SERVES 4

PUT the crabs in the freezer for 1 hour. Remove the top shell and bony tail flap from the underside of each crab, then remove the gills from both sides of the crab and the grit sac. Detach the claws and legs.

HEAT the butter in a large saucepan. Add the vegetables, bay leaf and thyme and cook over moderate heat for 3 minutes, without allowing the vegetables to colour. Add the crab claws, legs and body and cook for 5 minutes, or until the crab shells turn red. Add the tomato paste, brandy and white wine and simmer for 2 minutes, or until reduced by half.

ADD the stock and 500 ml (2 cups) water and bring to the boil. Reduce the heat and simmer for 5 minutes. Remove the shells and reserve the claws. Finely crush the shells with a pestle and mortar (or in a food processor with a little of the soup).

RETURN the crushed shells to the soup with the rice. Bring to the boil, reduce the heat, cover the pan and simmer for 30 minutes, or until the rice is very soft.

STRAIN the bisque into a clean saucepan through a fine sieve lined with damp muslin, pressing down firmly on the solids to extract all the cooking liquid. Add the cream and season with salt and cayenne, then gently reheat to serve. Ladle into warmed soup bowls and garnish, if you like, with the crab claws or some of the meat.

LEEK AND POTATO SOUP

LEEK AND POTATO SOUP CAN BE SERVED HOT OR CHILLED. IN ITS HOT FORM THE DISH IS TRADITIONALLY FRENCH. THE CHILLED VERSION, VICHYSSOISE, WAS THOUGHT TO HAVE BEEN FIRST SERVED AT THE RITZ-CARLTON HOTEL IN NEW YORK BY A FRENCH CHEF FROM VICHY.

50 g (1³/₄ oz) butter
1 onion, finely chopped
3 leeks, white part only, sliced
1 celery stalk, finely chopped
1 garlic clove, finely chopped
200 g (7 oz) potatoes, chopped
750 ml (3 cups) chicken stock
185 ml (³/₄ cup) cream
2 tablespoons chopped chives

SERVES 6

MELT the butter in a large saucepan and add the onion, leek, celery and garlic. Cover the pan and cook, stirring occasionally, over low heat for 15 minutes, or until the vegetables are softened but not browned. Add the potato and stock and bring to the boil.

REDUCE the heat and leave to simmer, covered, for 20 minutes. Allow to cool a little before puréeing in a blender or food processor. Return to the clean saucepan.

BRING the soup gently back to the boil and stir in the cream. Season with salt and white pepper and reheat without boiling. Serve hot or well chilled, garnished with chives.

Do not hurry the initial cooking of the leeks. The long cooking time over low heat is what gives them their sweet flavour.

WATERCRESS SOUP

30 g (1 oz) butter
1 onion, finely chopped
250 g (9 oz) potatoes, diced
625 ml (2¹/₂ cups) chicken stock
1 kg (2 lb 4 oz) watercress, trimmed
  and chopped
125 ml (¹/₂ cup) cream
125 ml (¹/₂ cup) milk
freshly grated nutmeg
2 tablespoons chopped chives

SERVES 4

MELT the butter in a large saucepan and add the onion. Cover the pan and cook over low heat until the onion is softened but not browned. Add the potato and chicken stock and simmer for 12 minutes, or until the potato is tender. Add the watercress and cook for 1 minute.

REMOVE FROM the heat and leave the soup to cool a little before pouring into a blender or food processor. Blend until smooth and return to the clean saucepan.

BRING the soup gently back to the boil and stir in the cream and milk. Season with nutmeg, salt and pepper and reheat without boiling. Serve garnished with chives.

WATERCRESS SOUP

A pavement café in Marseille.

Basil is more usually associated with Italy than France but, in fact, the herb originated not in Italy, but in India. It was introduced to Europe in the sixteenth century and is often used in southern French cooking as a perfect match for Provençal tomatoes and olive oil. It can be bought in pots or as bunches.

SOUPE AU PISTOU

PISTOU IS A PROVENÇAL MIXTURE OF GARLIC, BASIL AND PARMESAN MIXED TOGETHER WITH OLIVE OIL FROM THE SOUTH OF FRANCE. SIMILAR TO ITALIAN PESTO, IT IS THE TRADITIONAL ACCOMPANIMENT TO THIS SPRING VEGETABLE SOUP AND IS ADDED AT THE TABLE.

250 g (9 oz) dried haricot beans
2 teaspoons olive oil
1 onion, finely chopped
2 garlic cloves, crushed
1 celery stalk, chopped
3 carrots, diced
bouquet garni
4 potatoes, diced
150 g (5 1/2 oz) small green beans, chopped
500 ml (2 cups) chicken stock
3 tomatoes
4 zucchini (courgettes), diced
150 g (5 1/2 oz) vermicelli, broken into pieces
150 g (5 1/2 oz) peas, fresh or frozen

PISTOU
6 garlic cloves
85 g (3 oz) basil leaves
100 g (1 cup) grated Parmesan cheese
185 ml (3/4 cup) olive oil

SERVES 4

SOAK the haricot beans in cold water overnight, then drain, put in a saucepan and cover with cold water. Bring to the boil, then lower the heat and simmer for 1 hour, or until the beans are tender. Drain well.

TO MAKE the pistou, put the garlic, basil and Parmesan in a food processor or a mortar and pestle and process or pound until finely chopped. Slowly add the olive oil, with the motor running if you are using the food processor, or pounding constantly with the mortar and pestle, and mix thoroughly. Cover with plastic wrap and set aside.

HEAT the olive oil in a large saucepan, add the onion and garlic and cook over low heat for 5 minutes until softened but not browned. Add the celery, carrot and bouquet garni and cook for 10 minutes, stirring occasionally. Add the potato, green beans, chicken stock and 1.75 litres (7 cups) water and simmer for 10 minutes.

SCORE a cross in the top of each tomato. Plunge into boiling water for 20 seconds, then drain and peel the skin away from the cross. Chop the tomatoes finely, discarding the cores. Add to the soup with the zucchini, haricot beans, vermicelli and peas and cook for 10 minutes or until tender (if you are using frozen peas, add them at the last minute just to heat through). Season and serve with pistou on top.

BOURRIDE

THIS RICH FISH SOUP CAN BE SERVED IN A VARIETY OF WAYS. THE BREAD CAN BE PUT IN A DISH WITH THE FISH PILED ON TOP AND THE SOUP LADLED OVER, OR THE BROTH MAY BE SERVED WITH CROUTONS AND THE FISH EATEN SEPARATELY WITH BOILED POTATOES AS A MAIN COURSE.

GARLIC CROUTONS
1/2 stale baguette, sliced
60 ml (1/4 cup) olive oil
1 garlic clove, halved

AÏOLI
2 egg yolks
4 garlic cloves, crushed
3–5 teaspoons lemon juice
250 ml (1 cup) olive oil

STOCK
1/4 teaspoon saffron threads
1 litre (4 cups) dry white wine
1 leek, white part only, chopped
2 carrots, chopped
2 onions, chopped
2 long pieces orange zest
2 teaspoons fennel seeds
3 sprigs of thyme
2.5 kg (5 lb 8 oz) whole firm white
   fish such as monkfish, sea bass,
   cod, perch, sole or bream,
   filleted, skinned and cut into 4 cm
   (1 1/2 inch) pieces (reserve the
   trimmings)
3 egg yolks

SERVES 4

PREHEAT the oven to 160°C (315°F/Gas 2–3). Brush the bread with oil and bake for 10 minutes until crisp. Rub one side of each slice with garlic.

TO MAKE the aïoli, put the egg yolks, garlic and 3 teaspoons of the lemon juice in a mortar and pestle or food processor and pound or mix until light and creamy. Add the oil, drop by drop from the tip of a teaspoon, whisking constantly until it begins to thicken, then add the oil in a very thin stream. (If you're using a processor, pour in the oil in a thin stream with the motor running.) Season, add the remaining lemon juice and, if necessary, thin with a little warm water. Cover and refrigerate.

TO MAKE the stock, soak the saffron in a tablespoon of hot water for 15 minutes. Put the saffron, wine, leek, carrot, onion, orange zest, fennel seeds, thyme and fish trimmings in a large saucepan with 1 litre (4 cups) water. Cover and bring to the boil, then simmer for 20 minutes, skimming occasionally. Strain into a clean saucepan, pressing the solids with a wooden spoon to extract all the liquid. Bring the stock to a gentle simmer, add half the fish and poach for 5 minutes. Remove and keep warm while you cook the rest of the fish, then remove them from the pan and bring the stock back to the boil. Boil for 5 minutes, or until slightly reduced, and remove from the heat.

PUT HALF the aïoli and the yolks in a bowl and mix until smooth. Whisk in a ladleful of hot stock, then gradually add 5 ladlefuls, stirring constantly. Pour back into the pan holding the rest of the stock and whisk over low heat for 3–5 minutes, or until the soup is hot and slightly thicker (don't let it boil or it will curdle). Season with salt and pepper.

TO SERVE, put two garlic croutons in each bowl, top with a few pieces of fish and ladle over the hot soup. Serve the remaining aïoli separately.

Use slightly stale bread for the croutons. Rubbing with the cut side of the garlic will give them a mild flavour. Buy whole fish and cut them up yourself, keeping the trimmings. A flavoursome stock, made with fresh trimmings, is the basis of a good fish soup.

GARLIC SOUP

GARLIC SOUPS ARE SERVED THROUGHOUT FRANCE. IN PROVENCE, A SIMPLE SOUP OF GARLIC, HERBS AND OLIVE OIL IS KNOWN AS *AÏGO BOUÏDO*. THE SOUTHWEST VERSION, MADE WITH GOOSE FAT, IS CALLED *LE TOURAIN*. THIS SOUP IS GIVEN MORE SUBSTANCE WITH POTATO TO THICKEN IT.

2 bulbs of garlic, about 30 cloves,
   cloves separated
125 ml (1/2 cup) olive oil
125 g (41/2 oz) streaky bacon,
   finely chopped
1 floury potato, diced
1.5 litres (6 cups) chicken stock
   or water
bouquet garni
3 egg yolks

CHEESE CROUTONS
1/2 baguette or 1 ficelle, sliced
40 g (1/4 cup) grated Gruyère
   cheese

SERVES 4

SMASH the garlic with the flat side of a knife and peel. Heat 1 tablespoon of the oil in a large heavy-based saucepan and cook the bacon over moderate heat for 5 minutes without browning. Add the garlic and potato and cook for 5 minutes until softened. Add the stock and bouquet garni, bring to the boil and simmer for 30 minutes, or until the potato starts to dissolve into the soup.

PUT the egg yolks in a large bowl and pour in the remaining oil in a thin stream, whisking until thickened. Gradually whisk in the hot soup. Strain back into the saucepan, pressing to extract all the liquid, and heat gently without boiling. Season.

TO MAKE the cheese croutons, preheat the grill (broiler) and lightly toast the bread on both sides. Sprinkle with the cheese and grill (broil) until melted. Place a few croutons in each warm bowl and ladle the soup over the top.

Keeping the garlic cloves whole, rather than chopping them, gives a much sweeter flavour.

CABBAGE SOUP

100 g (1/2 cup) dried haricot beans
125 g (41/2 oz) bacon, cubed
40 g (11/2 oz) butter
1 carrot, sliced
1 onion, chopped
1 leek, white part only, roughly
   chopped
1 turnip, peeled and chopped
bouquet garni
1.25 litres (5 cups) chicken stock
400 g (14 oz) white cabbage, finely
   shredded

SERVES 4

SOAK the beans overnight in cold water. Drain, put in a saucepan and cover with cold water. Bring to the boil and simmer for 5 minutes, then drain. Put the bacon in the same saucepan, cover with water and simmer for 5 minutes. Drain and pat dry with paper towels.

MELT the butter in a large heavy-based saucepan, add the bacon and cook for 5 minutes, without browning. Add the beans, carrot, onion, leek and turnip and cook for 5 minutes. Add the bouquet garni and chicken stock and bring to the boil. Cover and simmer for 30 minutes. Add the cabbage, uncover and simmer for 30 minutes, or until the beans are tender. Remove the bouquet garni before serving and season to taste.

CABBAGE SOUP

HORS D'OEUVRES

A mortar and pestle is ideal for making tapenade, which should be a fairly rough paste. The name comes from *tapenado*, the Provençal word for caper.

AÏOLI

OFTEN REFERRED TO AS 'PROVENCE BUTTER', AÏOLI IS A SIMPLE BUT SUPERB GARLIC-FLAVOURED MAYONNAISE. IT IS SERVED WITH A SELECTION OF CRUDITÉS OR HOT VEGETABLES, POACHED CHICKEN, SNAILS OR FISH, AND IT CAN ALSO BE ADDED TO FISH SOUPS.

4 egg yolks
8 garlic cloves, crushed
1/2 teaspoon salt
2 tablespoons lemon juice
500 ml (2 cups) olive oil

CRUDITÉS
6 baby carrots, trimmed with stalks
   left on
6 asparagus spears, trimmed and
   blanched
6 French beans, trimmed and
   blanched
6 button mushrooms, halved
1 yellow capsicum (pepper),
   seeded and cut into batons
1 red capsicum (pepper), seeded
   and cut into batons
6 cauliflower florets
1 fennel bulb, cut into batons

SERVES 6

PUT the egg yolks, garlic, salt and half the lemon juice in a mortar and pestle or food processor and pound or mix until light and creamy. Add the oil, drop by drop from the tip of a teaspoon, whisking constantly until it begins to thicken, then add the oil in a very thin stream. (If you're using a processor, pour in the oil in a thin stream with the motor running.) Season, add the remaining lemon juice and, if necessary, thin with a little warm water.

ARRANGE the crudités around a large platter and serve the aïoli in a bowl in the centre. You can keep aïoli sealed in a sterilized jar in the fridge. It will last for up to 3 weeks.

TAPENADE

300 g (10 1/2 oz) black olives, pitted
3 tablespoons capers, rinsed
8 anchovies
1 garlic clove, crushed
185 ml (3/4 cup) olive oil
1 tablespoon lemon juice
2 teaspoons Dijon mustard
1 teaspoon chopped thyme
1 tablespoon chopped parsley

SERVES 6

POUND TOGETHER the olives, capers, anchovies and garlic, either using a mortar and pestle or a food processor. Add the olive oil, lemon juice, mustard and herbs and pound or process again until you have a fairly rough paste.

SERVE with bread or crudités for dipping. Can be kept, covered, in the fridge for several days.

TAPENADE

LEEKS A LA GRECQUE

A LA GRECQUE REFERS TO THE GREEK STYLE OF COOKING, USING OLIVE OIL, LEMON, HERBS AND SPICES. THESE INGREDIENTS THAT ARE SO READILY FOUND IN THE DUSTY GREEK HILLSIDES ARE EQUALLY AT HOME IN THE MORE VERDANT LANDSCAPE OF FRANCE.

60 ml (1/4 cup) extra virgin olive oil
30 ml (1 fl oz) white wine
1 tablespoon tomato paste (purée)
1/4 teaspoon sugar
1 bay leaf
1 sprig of thyme
1 garlic clove, crushed
4 coriander seeds, crushed
4 peppercorns
8 small leeks, trimmed
1 teaspoon lemon juice
1 tablespoon chopped parsley

SERVES 4

PUT the oil, wine, tomato paste, sugar, bay leaf, thyme, garlic, coriander, peppercorns and 250 ml (1 cup) water in a large non-aluminium frying pan. Bring to the boil, cover and simmer for 5 minutes.

ADD the leeks in a single layer and bring to simmering point. Reduce the heat, cover the pan again and cook for 20–30 minutes, or until the leeks are tender (pierce with a fine skewer). Lift out the leeks and put them in a serving dish.

ADD the lemon juice to the cooking liquid and boil rapidly until the liquid is slightly syrupy. Remove the bay leaf, thyme and peppercorns. Season with salt and pour over the leeks. Serve the leeks cold, sprinkled with chopped parsley.

Add the leeks to the simmering liquid and cook in a single layer.

MUSHROOMS A LA GRECQUE

2 tomatoes
80 ml (1/3 cup) extra virgin olive oil
60 ml (1/4 cup) white wine
2 French shallots, finely chopped
1 garlic clove, crushed
6 coriander seeds, lightly crushed
1 bay leaf
1 sprig of thyme
500 g (1 lb 2 oz) button mushrooms
2 teaspoons lemon juice
pinch of sugar
1 tablespoon chopped parsley

SERVES 4

SCORE a cross in the top of each tomato. Plunge into boiling water for 20 seconds, then drain and peel the skin away from the cross. Chop the tomatoes, discarding the cores.

PUT the oil, wine, tomato, shallots, garlic, coriander seeds, bay leaf, thyme and 250 ml (1 cup) water in a non-aluminium saucepan. Bring to the boil, cover and simmer for 10 minutes. Uncover the pan, add the mushrooms and simmer for a further 10 minutes, stirring occasionally. Lift out the mushrooms with a slotted spoon and put them in a serving dish.

BOIL the cooking liquid rapidly until you have only about 250 ml (1 cup) left. Remove the bay leaf and thyme. Add the lemon juice and season with salt, pepper and the sugar. Pour the liquid over the mushrooms and leave to cool. Serve the mushrooms cold, sprinkled with chopped parsley.

MUSHROOMS A LA GRECQUE

ASPARAGUS WITH HOLLANDAISE SAUCE

24 asparagus spears

HOLLANDAISE SAUCE
2 egg yolks
2 teaspoons lemon juice
90 g (3¼ oz) unsalted butter, cut
    into cubes

SERVES 4

WASH the asparagus and remove the woody ends (hold each spear at both ends and bend it gently—it will snap at its natural breaking point). Cook the asparagus in a frying pan of simmering salted water for 4 minutes, or until just tender. Drain, then cool under cold running water.

TO MAKE the hollandaise sauce, put the egg yolks and lemon juice in a saucepan over very low heat. Whisk continuously, adding the butter piece by piece until the sauce thickens. Do not overheat or the eggs will scramble. Season.

(ALTERNATIVELY, put the eggs yolks, salt and pepper in a blender and mix together. Heat the lemon juice and butter together until boiling and then, with the motor running, pour onto the yolks in a steady stream.)

ARRANGE a few asparagus spears on each plate and spoon the hollandaise over the top.

Pound the anchoïade mixture to a coarse paste and then add a little extra olive oil to give it a spreadable consistency.

ANCHOÏADE

COLLIOURE ON THE SOUTH COAST IS THE HOME OF ANCHOVY FISHING IN FRANCE AND IT IS FROM THE SOUTH THAT THIS PUNGENT ANCHOVY PASTE HAILS. IT CAN BE SERVED AS A DIP, STIRRED INTO DRESSINGS AND STEWS, OR SPREAD ON BREAD, FISH AND CHICKEN AND THEN GRILLED (BROILED).

85 g (3 oz) anchovy fillets in oil
2 garlic cloves
14 black olives, pitted
1 small tomato
1 teaspoon thyme leaves
3 teaspoons chopped parsley
olive oil
8 slices baguette

SERVES 4

PUT the anchovies (with their oil), garlic, olives, tomato, thyme, 1 teaspoon chopped parsley and a generous grinding of black pepper in a mortar and pestle or food processor and pound or mix until you have a coarse paste. Add a little extra olive oil if the paste is very thick—it should have a spreadable consistency.

PREHEAT the grill (broiler) and toast the baguette slices on both sides until golden brown. Spread the anchoïade over the baguette and sprinkle with the remaining parsley.

ANCHOÏADE

FRANCE'S BOULANGERIES are named after *boules,* the round balls of dough found in bakeries. Every village in France must by law have somewhere selling bread and in most villages the boulangerie will bake bread twice daily. If there is no boulangerie, the general village shop will display a *'depôt de pain'* sign showing that it sells bread brought to the 'depot' daily. A boulangerie may also double-up as a patisserie

BREAD

BREAD IS AN ESSENTIAL PART OF FRENCH LIFE. EATEN WITH EVERY MEAL, BREAD IS BOUGHT DAILY, OR EVEN TWICE DAILY, AND BY LAW, EVERY VILLAGE IN FRANCE MUST HAVE A SHOP MAKING OR SELLING BREAD.

Breads are sold not only by the loaf (*la pièce*) but also by weight, perpetuating the tradition of buying just enough bread for each meal or day. Boulangeries bake twice daily so that people can have the freshest bread possible, especially as a baguette made of just wheat flour, yeast and salt begins to go stale after only a few hours.

Bread has been the staple of the French diet since the Middle Ages. The first loaves were large and coarse, made from a mix of flours and unsalted because of the high price of salt. Not until the seventeenth century was white bread invented when a method for removing bran was discovered.

THE BAGUETTE

The baguette is seen as a symbol of France, but many Frenchmen see it instead as a symbol of Paris. Invented in the nineteenth century and based on Viennese bread, it was made from white flour and a sourdough starter, then rolled up into a slim, light loaf with lots of crust. Paris, always a great consumer of bread due to its place in the centre of the Beauce wheat plains, immediately took to the new loaf, though it was not until the twentieth century that it became truly popular in rural France. The best baguettes have a crisp, golden outside, with the score marks rising above the crust.

and all boulangeries bake croissants, brioche and *pain au chocolat* to be eaten with a *café au lait* for a simple French breakfast. Bread is also made by hand by small artisan producers and sold in the markets, along with specialities such as the pastries being eaten as a snack *(le goûter)* by two girls in a market in Provence, and also traditional breads such as the *pain au levain* sold from a van in a Lyon market.

TYPES OF BREADS

Although the elegant baguette is still France's most popular bread, the more rustic and nutritious *pain de campagne* is growing in popularity, as are other loaves made from barley and rye. These country-style breads often use a *levain* (sourdough starter) rather than yeast. Sourdough breads have a long production time, but they do keep for a few days rather than going stale quickly like baguettes. These loaves may also be baked in a wood-fired oven, which adds a smoky taste.

A real baguette is actually a certain weight and size (about 70 cm/28 inches in length and 250 g/9 oz in weight) and not all long loaves are baguettes. A flûte is heavier and longer, and a ficelle thinner and lighter, though all are made in the same way. A long, thin *pain au levain* (sourdough bread) may also be labelled as a baguette, as the shape is now so recognizable that the name covers many things.

THE SOURDOUGH BREADS shown here are made by the French *levain* system, using a living sourdough starter in which the yeasts that cause the bread to rise are organic. The starter ferments for at least a few days to give the bread its tangy taste.

41

CELERIAC REMOULADE

juice of 1 lemon
2 celeriac, trimmed and peeled
2 tablespoons capers
5 cornichons, chopped
2 tablespoons finely chopped
   parsley

MUSTARD MAYONNAISE
2 egg yolks
1 tablespoon white wine vinegar or
   lemon juice
1 tablespoon Dijon mustard
125 ml (1/2 cup) light olive oil

SERVES 4

PLACE 1 litre (4 cups) cold water in a large bowl and add half the lemon juice. Roughly grate the celeriac and then place in the acidulated water. Bring a saucepan of water to the boil and add the remaining lemon juice. Drain the celeriac and add to the water. After 1 minute, drain and cool under running water. Pat dry with paper towels.

TO MAKE the mustard mayonnaise, put the egg yolks, vinegar or lemon juice and mustard in a bowl or food processor and whisk together. Add the oil, drop by drop from the tip of a teaspoon, whisking constantly until it begins to thicken, then add the oil in a very thin stream. (If you're using a processor, pour in the oil in a thin stream with the motor running.) Season and, if necessary, thin with a little warm water.

TOSS the celeriac with the mayonnaise, capers, cornichons and parsley. Serve with bread.

Once the mayonnaise has started to thicken, you can add the oil in a thin stream, whisking constantly.

POTATO SALAD

POTATO VARIETIES CONTAIN VARYING AMOUNTS OF STARCH, MAKING THEM EITHER 'WAXY' OR 'FLOURY'. WAXY OR ALL-PURPOSE VARIETIES, SUCH AS DESIREE, ARE LOWER IN STARCH AND HOLD THEIR SHAPE WHEN COOKED, MAKING THEM BETTER FOR SALADS.

4 large waxy potatoes, cubed
3 celery stalks
1 red capsicum (pepper)
1 tablespoon olive oil
80 ml (1/3 cup) mayonnaise
   (page 286)
juice of 1 lemon
1 1/2 tablespoons chopped parsley

SERVES 4

PUT the potatoes in a large saucepan, cover with cold water and cook for 15 minutes, or until just tender (don't allow them to overcook). Refresh under cold water and drain.

STRING the celery stalks and cut them into very small dice. Cut the capsicum in half, remove the seeds and dice finely.

PUT the potato, celery and capsicum in a bowl, add the olive oil, mayonnaise, lemon juice and parsley and toss well. Season well before serving.

POTATO SALAD

RAW OYSTERS

24 oysters in their shells
1 French shallot, finely chopped
2 tablespoons red wine vinegar
1 lemon, cut into wedges

SERVES 4

SHUCK the oysters by holding each one, rounded side down, in a cloth in your left hand. Using an oyster knife, carefully wiggle the point of the knife between the two shells and, keeping the blade flat, run the knife across the top shell to sever the muscle. Pull off the top shell and loosen the oyster from the bottom shell, being careful not to lose any liquid. Nestle the opened oysters on a bed of crushed ice or rock salt on a large platter (this will keep them steady).

MIX the shallot with the red wine vinegar and some black pepper in a small bowl. Put this in the centre of the platter and arrange the lemon wedges around the oysters. Serve with slices of rye bread and butter.

RAW OYSTERS

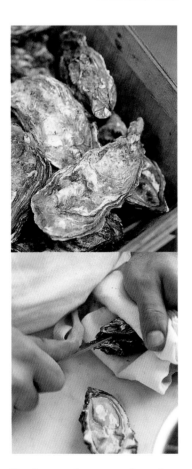

OYSTERS MORNAY

24 oysters in their shells
50 g (1³/₄ oz) butter
1 French shallot, finely chopped
30 g (¹/₄ cup) plain (all-purpose) flour
375 ml (1¹/₂ cups) milk
pinch of nutmeg
¹/₂ bay leaf
35 g (¹/₄ cup) grated Gruyère cheese
25 g (¹/₄ cup) grated Parmesan cheese, plus a little extra for grilling (broiling)

SERVES 6

SHUCK the oysters, reserving all the liquid. Strain the liquid into a saucepan. Rinse the oysters to remove any bits of shell. Wash and dry the shells.

MELT 30 g (1 oz) of the butter in a saucepan, add the shallot and cook, stirring, for 3 minutes. Stir in the flour to make a roux and stir over very low heat for 3 minutes without allowing the roux to brown. Remove from the heat and add the milk gradually, stirring after each addition until smooth. Return to the heat, add the nutmeg and bay leaf and simmer for 5 minutes. Strain through a fine sieve into a clean pan.

HEAT the oyster liquid in the saucepan to a simmer (add a little water if you need more liquid). Add the oysters and poach for 30 seconds, then lift them out with a slotted spoon and place them back into their shells. Stir the cooking liquid into the sauce. Add the cheeses and remaining butter and stir until they have melted into the sauce. Season with salt and pepper. Preheat the grill (broiler).

SPOON a little sauce over each oyster, sprinkle with Parmesan and place under the hot grill (broiler) for a couple of minutes, or until golden.

To store oysters, wrap them in a damp cloth and refrigerate in the salad compartment for up to 3 days. Eat oysters that have been shucked immediately.

ARTICHOKES VINAIGRETTE

THIS IS THE CLASSIC WAY TO SERVE ARTICHOKES: YOU JUST NEED TO MAKE SURE YOU BUY THE BEST
ONES AVAILABLE. SMALLER ARTICHOKES CAN ALSO BE PREPARED IN THIS FASHION, BUT CUT THEM
INTO QUARTERS AND SERVE WITH THE DRESSING RATHER THAN REMOVING THE LEAVES ONE BY ONE.

juice of 1 lemon
4 globe artichokes

VINAIGRETTE
5 tablespoons olive oil
2 spring onions (scallions), finely
   chopped
2 tablespoons white wine
2 tablespoons white wine vinegar
1/4 teaspoon Dijon mustard
pinch of sugar
1 tablespoon finely chopped
   parsley

SERVES 4

TO PREPARE the artichokes, bring a large
saucepan of salted water to the boil and add the
lemon juice. Break the stalks from the artichokes,
pulling out any strings at the same time, and then
trim the bases flat. Add the artichokes to the
water and put a small plate on top of them to
keep them submerged. Cook at a simmer for
25–30 minutes, or until a leaf from the base
comes away easily. (The base will be tender when
pierced with a skewer.) Cool quickly under cold
running water, then drain upside down on a tray.

TO MAKE the vinaigrette, heat 1 tablespoon of
the oil in a small saucepan, add the spring onion
and cook over low heat for 2 minutes. Leave to
cool a little, then add the white wine, vinegar,
mustard and sugar and gradually whisk in the
remaining oil. Season well with salt and pepper
and stir in half the parsley.

PLACE an artichoke on each plate and gently
prise it open a little. Spoon the dressing over the
top, allowing it to drizzle into the artichoke and
around the plate. Pour the remaining dressing into
a small bowl for people to dip the leaves. Sprinkle
each artichoke with a little parsley.

EAT the leaves one by one, dipping them in the
vinaigrette and scraping the flesh off the leaves
between your teeth. When you reach the middle,
pull off any really small leaves and then use a
teaspoon to remove the furry choke. Once you've
got rid of the choke, you can eat the tender base
or 'heart' of the artichoke.

Whisking the remaining oil into
the vinaigrette.

PETITS FARCIS

THIS WONDERFUL DISH FROM PROVENCE MAKES GOOD USE OF THE REGION'S ABUNDANCE OF
GARDEN PRODUCE AND THE STUFFING CAN INCLUDE ANY HERBS, MEAT OR CHEESES AT HAND. SERVE
HOT OR COLD WITH BREAD FOR A SIMPLE SUMMER LUNCH.

Hollow out the vegetables with
a spoon and brush the edges
with a little oil before filling with
the stuffing.

2 small eggplants (aubergines),
   halved lengthways
2 small zucchini (courgettes), halved
   lengthways
4 tomatoes
2 small red capsicums (peppers),
   halved lengthways and seeded
4 tablespoons olive oil
2 red onions, chopped
2 garlic cloves, crushed
250 g (9 oz) minced (ground) pork
250 g (9 oz) minced (ground) veal
50 g (1³/4 oz) tomato paste (purée)
80 ml (1/3 cup) white wine
2 tablespoons chopped parsley
50 g (1/2 cup) grated Parmesan
   cheese
80 g (1 cup) fresh breadcrumbs

SERVES 4

PREHEAT the oven to 180°C (350°F/Gas 4).
Grease a large roasting tin with oil. Use a spoon
to hollow out the centres of the eggplants and
zucchini, leaving a border around the edge. Chop
the flesh finely.

CUT the tops from the tomatoes (don't throw
away the tops). Use a spoon to hollow out the
centres, catching the juice in a bowl, and chop
the flesh roughly. Arrange the vegetables,
including the red capsicum, in the roasting tin.
Brush the edges of the eggplants and zucchini
with a little of the oil. Pour 125 ml (1/2 cup) water
into the roasting tin.

HEAT HALF the oil in a large frying pan. Cook
the onion and garlic for 3 minutes, or until they
have softened. Add the pork and veal and stir for
5 minutes until the meat browns, breaking up any
lumps with the back of a fork. Add the chopped
eggplant and zucchini and cook for a further
3 minutes. Add the tomato pulp and juice, tomato
paste and wine. Cook, stirring occasionally, for
10 minutes.

REMOVE the frying pan from the heat and stir in
the parsley, Parmesan and breadcrumbs. Season
well with salt and pepper. Spoon the mixture into
the vegetables. Place the tops back on the
tomatoes. Sprinkle the vegetables with the
remaining oil and bake for 45 minutes, or until the
vegetables are tender.

MILLEFEUILLE OF LEEKS AND POACHED EGGS

MILLEFEUILLE MEANS 'A THOUSAND LEAVES' AND REFERS TO THE MANY LAYERS OF THE PUFF PASTRY.
YOU CAN EITHER USE THE RECIPE IN THIS BOOK OR 350 GRAMS (12 OUNCES) READY-MADE PUFF
PASTRY. MAKE SURE YOU USE THE FRESHEST EGGS YOU CAN FIND.

1/2 quantity puff pastry (page 281)
1 egg, lightly beaten
3 leeks, white part only
30 g (1 oz) butter
4 eggs

BEURRE BLANC
2 French shallots, finely chopped
1 tablespoon butter
3 tablespoons white wine
185 ml (3/4 cup) chicken stock
175 g (6 oz) unsalted butter, chilled
and diced

SERVES 4

PREHEAT the oven to 190°C (375°F/Gas 5). Roll
out the pastry on a lightly floured surface to make
a 24 x 12 cm (9 1/2 x 5 inch) rectangle. Chill for
10 minutes and then cut into four equal triangles.
Trim the edges so that they are straight. Place the
triangles on a damp baking tray, lightly brush with
the beaten egg and bake for 15 minutes, or until
puffed and golden brown. Slice the triangles in
half horizontally and use a spoon to remove any
uncooked dough from the inside.

CUT the leeks in half and then into thin julienne
strips. Melt the butter in a frying pan, add the
leeks and cook, stirring, for 10 minutes or until
they are tender. Season with salt.

TO POACH the eggs, bring a pan of water to the
boil. Crack an egg into a ramekin, reduce the heat
and slide the egg into the simmering water. Poach
for 3 minutes, then remove carefully with a slotted
spoon and drain on paper towels. Poach all the
eggs in the same way.

TO MAKE the beurre blanc, fry the shallots gently
in the butter until they are tender but not
browned. Add the wine and bubble in the pan
until reduced by half. Add the stock and continue
cooking until reduced by a third. Add the butter,
piece by piece, whisking continuously until the
sauce thickens—take care not to overheat. You
may need to move the pan on and off the heat to
keep the temperature even. Season the beurre
blanc with salt and white pepper.

ARRANGE the base triangles of pastry on a
serving dish, top each one with a spoonful of
warm leek, then a poached egg and a little beurre
blanc. Cover with the pastry tops and serve with
the beurre blanc drizzled around or on the side.

Cook the julienned leek in butter
until it is tender. When making
the beurre blanc, take care not to
overheat the sauce or the butter
will melt too quickly and not form
an emulsion.

SMOKED TROUT GOUGÈRE

FOR A GOUGÈRE, CHOUX PASTRY IS TRADITIONALLY PIPED INTO A CIRCULAR OR OVAL SHAPE AND FILLED WITH A SAVOURY MIXTURE. IF YOU PREFER, THE PASTRY CAN ALSO BE MADE INTO SMALL CHOUX BUNS, SPLIT OPEN AND THE FILLING SPOONED INTO THE CENTRES.

Spoon the choux pastry around the edge of the baking dish and bake until well risen. To remove the bone from the trout, simply lift off the top fillet and then lift the bone away cleanly.

80 g (3 oz) butter
125 g (1 cup) plain (all-purpose) flour, sifted twice
1/4 teaspoon paprika
3 large eggs, beaten
100 g (3/4 cup) grated Gruyère cheese

FILLING
400 g (14 oz) smoked trout
100 g (3 1/2 oz) watercress, trimmed
30 g (1 oz) butter
1 tablespoon plain (all-purpose) flour
300 ml (10 1/2 fl oz) milk

SERVES 4

PREHEAT the oven to 200°C (400°F/Gas 6) and put a baking tray on the top shelf to heat up.

MELT the butter with 185 ml (3/4 cup) water in a saucepan, then bring it to a rolling boil. Remove from the heat and sift in all the flour and the paprika. Return to the heat and beat continuously with a wooden spoon to make a smooth shiny paste that comes away from the side of the pan. Cool for a few minutes. Beat in the eggs one at a time, until shiny and smooth—the mixture should drop off the spoon but not be too runny. Stir in two-thirds of the cheese.

SPOON the dough round the edge of a shallow, lightly greased baking dish. Put this in the oven on the hot tray and cook for 45–50 minutes, or until the choux is well risen and browned.

MEANWHILE, to make the filling, peel the skin off the trout and lift off the top fillet. Pull out the bone. Break the trout into large flakes. Wash the watercress and put in a large saucepan with just the water clinging to the leaves. Cover the pan and steam the watercress for 2 minutes, or until just wilted. Drain, cool and squeeze with your hands to get rid of the excess liquid. Roughly chop the watercress.

MELT the butter in a saucepan, stir in the flour to make a roux and cook, stirring, for 3 minutes over very low heat without allowing the roux to brown. Remove from the heat and add the milk gradually, stirring after each addition until smooth. Return to the heat and simmer for 3 minutes. Stir in the smoked trout and watercress and season well.

SPOON the trout filling into the centre of the cooked choux pastry and return to the oven for 10 minutes, then serve immediately.

PROVENÇAL TART

PASTRY
250 g (2 cups) plain (all-purpose)
   flour
150 g (5¹/₂ oz) butter, diced
1 egg yolk, beaten

2 tablespoons olive oil
1 large white onion, finely chopped
10 tomatoes (or 2 x 400 g/14 oz
   tins chopped tomatoes)
1 teaspoon tomato paste (purée)
2 garlic cloves, finely chopped
1 tablespoon roughly chopped
   oregano, plus a few whole leaves
   to garnish
1 red capsicum (pepper)
1 yellow capsicum (pepper)
6 anchovies, halved
12 pitted olives
drizzle of olive oil

SERVES 6

TO MAKE the pastry, sift the flour into a bowl, add the butter and rub in with your fingertips until the mixture resembles breadcrumbs. Add the egg yolk and about 2–3 teaspoons cold water and mix with the blade of a palette knife until the dough starts to come together. Bring it together with your hands and shape into a ball. Wrap in plastic wrap and put in the fridge for at least 30 minutes.

HEAT the oil in a frying pan, add the onion, cover and cook over very low heat for 20 minutes, stirring often, until softened but not browned.

SCORE a cross in the top of each tomato. Plunge into boiling water for 20 seconds, then drain and peel the skin away from the cross. Chop the tomatoes, discarding the cores. Add the tomato, tomato paste, garlic and oregano to the frying pan and simmer, uncovered, for 20 minutes, stirring occasionally. Once the tomato is soft and the mixture has become a paste, leave to cool.

ROLL OUT the pastry to fit a 34 x 26 cm (13¹/₂ x 10¹/₂ inch) shallow baking tray. Prick the pastry gently all over, without piercing right through. Cover with plastic wrap and chill for 30 minutes. Preheat the oven to 200°C (400°F/Gas 6) and preheat the grill (broiler).

CUT the capsicums in half, remove the seeds and membrane and place, skin side up, under the hot grill until the skin blackens and blisters. Leave to cool before peeling away the skin. Cut the capsicums into thin strips.

LINE the pastry shell with a crumpled piece of greaseproof paper and fill with baking beads (use dried beans or rice if you don't have beads). Blind bake the pastry for 10 minutes, remove the paper and beads and bake for a further 3–5 minutes, or until the pastry is just cooked but still very pale. Reduce the oven to 180°C (350°F/Gas 4).

SPREAD the tomato over the pastry, then scatter with capsicum. Arrange the anchovies and olives over the top. Brush with olive oil and bake for 25 minutes. Scatter with oregano leaves to serve.

Simmer the filling until the tomato is so soft that it forms a paste.

PISSALADIÈRE

PISSALADIÈRE TAKES ITS NAME FROM *PISSALAT*, PURÉED ANCHOVIES. IT CAN VARY IN ITS TOPPING FROM ONIONS AND ANCHOVIES TO ONIONS, TOMATOES AND ANCHOVIES OR SIMPLY ANCHOVIES PURÉED WITH GARLIC. TRADITIONAL TO NICE, IT CAN BE MADE WITH A BREAD OR PASTRY BASE.

40 g (1¹/₂ oz) butter
1 tablespoon olive oil
1.5 kg (3 lb 5 oz) onions, thinly
    sliced
2 tablespoons thyme leaves
1 quantity bread dough (page 277)
1 tablespoon olive oil
16 anchovies, halved lengthways
24 pitted olives

SERVES 6

MELT the butter with the olive oil in a saucepan and add the onion and half the thyme. Cover the saucepan and cook over low heat for 45 minutes, stirring occasionally, until the onion is softened but not browned. Season and cool. Preheat the oven to 200°C (400°F/Gas 6).

ROLL OUT the bread dough to roughly fit an oiled 34 x 26 cm (13¹/₂ x 10¹/₂ inch) shallow baking tray. Brush with the olive oil, then spread with the onion.

LAY the anchovies in a lattice pattern over the onion and arrange the olives in the lattice diamonds. Bake for 20 minutes, or until the dough is cooked and lightly browned. Sprinkle with the remaining thyme leaves and cut into squares. Serve hot or warm.

Spread the softened onion over the bread base and then arrange the anchovies over the top in the traditional lattice pattern.

TARTE FLAMBÉE

TARTE FLAMBÉE IS THE ALSATIAN VERSION OF THE PIZZA. IT IS COOKED QUICKLY AT A VERY HIGH TEMPERATURE IN A WOOD-FIRED OVEN AND TAKES ITS NAME FROM THE FACT THAT THE EDGE OF THE DOUGH OFTEN CAUGHT FIRE IN THE INTENSE HEAT OF THE OVEN.

2 tablespoons olive oil
2 white onions, sliced
100 g (3¹/₂ oz) cream cheese or
    curd cheese
185 ml (³/₄ cup) fromage frais
200 g (7 oz) piece of bacon, cut
    into lardons
1 quantity bread dough (page 277)

SERVES 6

PREHEAT the oven to 230°C (450°F/Gas 8). Heat the olive oil in a saucepan and fry the onion until softened but not browned. Beat the cream or curd cheese with the fromage frais and then add the onion and bacon and season well.

ROLL OUT the bread dough into a rectangle about 3 mm (¹/₈ inch) thick—the dough needs to be thin, like a pizza—and place on an oiled baking tray. Fold the edge of the dough over to make a slight rim. Spread the topping over the dough, right up to the rim, and bake for 10–15 minutes, or until the dough is crisp and cooked and the topping browned. Cut into squares to serve.

TARTE FLAMBÉE

EGGS & CHEESE

HAM, MUSHROOM AND CHEESE CRÊPES

Once the crêpe starts to come away from the side of the pan, turn it over.

1 quantity crêpe batter (page 282)
1 tablespoon butter
150 g (5¹/2 oz) mushrooms, sliced
2 tablespoons cream
165 g (1¹/4 cups) grated Gruyère cheese
100 g (3¹/2 oz) ham, chopped

SERVES 6

HEAT a large crêpe or frying pan and grease with a little butter or oil. Pour in enough batter to coat the base of the pan in a thin even layer and tip out any excess. Cook over moderate heat for about a minute, or until the crêpe starts to come away from the side of the pan. Turn the crêpe and cook on the other side for 1 minute or until lightly golden. Stack the crêpes on a plate, with pieces of greaseproof paper between them, and cover with plastic wrap while you cook the rest of the batter to make six large crêpes.

PREHEAT the oven to 180°C (350°F/Gas 4). Heat the butter in a frying pan, add the mushrooms, season well and cook, stirring, for 5 minutes, or until all the liquid from the mushrooms has evaporated. Stir in the cream, cheese and ham.

LAY one crêpe on a board or work surface. Top with about a sixth of the filling and fold the crêpe into quarters. Place it on a baking tray and then fill and fold the remaining crêpes. Bake for 5 minutes and then serve immediately.

CERVELLE DE CANUT

CERVELLE DE CANUT IS A LYONNAIS DISH. THE NAME MEANS 'SILK WEAVERS' BRAINS' (APPARENTLY SILK WEAVERS WERE CONSIDERED TO BE QUITE STUPID). DEPENDING ON THE TYPE OF CHEESE THAT YOU USE, THE DISH CAN BE SMOOTH AND CREAMY OR RATHER MORE COARSE.

500 g (1 lb 2 oz) fromage blanc or curd cheese
2 tablespoons olive oil
1 garlic clove, finely chopped
2 tablespoons chopped chervil
4 tablespoons chopped parsley
2 tablespoons chopped chives
1 tablespoon chopped tarragon
4 French shallots, finely chopped

SERVES 8

BEAT the fromage blanc or curd cheese with a wooden spoon, then add the olive oil and garlic and beat it into the cheese. Add the herbs and shallots and mix together well. Season and serve with pieces of toast or bread, perhaps after dessert as you would cheese and biscuits.

CERVELLE DE CANUT

OMELETTE AUX FINES HERBES

THE OMELETTE IS WONDERFULLY ACCOMMODATING TO PERSONAL TASTE—IT CAN BE FOLDED, ROLLED OR LEFT FLAT, COOKED ON ONE SIDE OR BOTH. THIS FOLDED OMELETTE IS TRADITIONALLY *BAVEUSE* (CREAMY) IN THE MIDDLE AND COOKED ON ONE SIDE ONLY BEFORE BEING FOLDED.

1 tablespoon butter
2 French shallots, finely chopped
1 garlic clove, crushed
2 tablespoons chopped parsley
2 tablespoons chopped basil
$1/2$ tablespoon chopped tarragon
2 tablespoons double (thick/heavy) cream
8 eggs, lightly beaten
oil

SERVES 4

MELT the butter in a frying pan and cook the shallots and garlic over low heat until tender. Stir in the herbs and then tip into a bowl. Mix in the cream and eggs and season well.

HEAT A LITTLE oil in a non-stick frying pan. Pour a quarter of the batter into the pan and cook gently, constantly pulling the set egg around the edge of the pan into the centre, until the omelette is set and browned underneath and the top is just cooked. Fold the omelette into three and slide it out of the pan onto a plate with the seam underneath. Serve hot, for someone else to eat while you cook up the remaining three omelettes.

When the omelette is set and browned underneath, fold it in three so the inside stays creamy.

CROQUE MONSIEUR

80 g (3 oz) unsalted butter
1 tablespoon plain (all-purpose) flour
185 ml ($3/4$ cup) milk
$1/2$ teaspoon Dijon mustard
1 egg yolk
grated nutmeg
12 slices white bread
6 slices ham
130 g (1 cup) grated Gruyère cheese

SERVES 6

MELT 20 g ($3/4$ oz) of the butter in a saucepan, add the flour and stir over low heat for 3 minutes. Slowly add the milk and mustard, whisking constantly. Leave to simmer until the mixture has thickened and reduced by about a third. Remove from the heat and stir in the egg yolk. Season with salt, pepper and nutmeg and leave to cool completely.

PLACE HALF the bread slices on a baking tray. Top each piece of bread with a slice of ham, then with some of the sauce, then Gruyère and finally with another piece of bread. Melt half the remaining butter in a large frying pan and fry the sandwiches on both sides until they are golden brown, adding the remaining butter when you need it. Cut each sandwich in half to serve.

CROQUE MONSIEUR

Finely grate the cheese for soufflés so that it melts quickly without forming bubbles of oil.

Round zucchini (courgettes) are used in the same way as the more common long variety.

ZUCCHINI SOUFFLÉ

SOUFFLÉS HAVE DEVELOPED A REPUTATION AS UNPREDICTABLE CREATIONS, BUT THEY ARE NOT HARD TO MAKE. THE SECRET LIES IN BEATING THE EGG WHITES TO THE RIGHT STIFFNESS AND SERVING THE SOUFFLÉ STRAIGHT FROM OVEN TO TABLE. YOU COULD USE BROCCOLI INSTEAD OF ZUCCHINI.

1 tablespoon butter, melted
1 1/2 tablespoons dried breadcrumbs
350 g (12 oz) zucchini (courgettes), chopped
125 ml (1/2 cup) milk
30 g (1 oz) butter
30 g (1/4 cup) plain (all-purpose) flour
85 g (3 oz) Gruyère or Parmesan cheese, finely grated
3 spring onions (scallions), finely chopped
4 eggs, separated

SERVES 4

BRUSH a 1.5 litre (6 cup) soufflé dish with the melted butter, then tip the breadcrumbs into the dish. Rotate the dish to coat the side completely with breadcrumbs. Tip out the excess breadcrumbs.

COOK the zucchini in boiling water for 8 minutes until tender. Drain and then put the zucchini in a food processor with the milk and mix until smooth. Alternatively, mash the zucchini with the milk and then press it through a sieve with a wooden spoon. Preheat the oven to 180°C (350°F/Gas 4).

MELT the butter in a heavy-based saucepan and stir in the flour to make a roux. Cook, stirring, for 2 minutes over low heat without allowing the roux to brown. Remove from the heat and add the zucchini purée, stirring until smooth. Return to the heat and bring to the boil. Simmer, stirring, for 3 minutes, then remove from the heat. Pour into a bowl, add the cheese and spring onion and season well. Mix until smooth, then beat in the egg yolks until smooth again.

WHISK the egg whites in a clean dry bowl until they form soft peaks. Spoon a quarter of the egg white onto the soufflé mixture and quickly but lightly fold it in, to loosen the mixture. Lightly fold in the remaining egg white. Pour into the soufflé dish and run your thumb around the inside rim of the dish, about 2 cm (3/4 inch) into the soufflé mixture (try not to wipe off the breadcrumbs and butter). This helps the soufflé rise without sticking.

BAKE for 45 minutes, or until the soufflé is well risen and wobbles slightly when tapped. Test with a skewer through a crack in the side of the soufflé—the skewer should come out clean or slightly moist. If the skewer is slightly moist, by the time the soufflé makes it to the table it will be cooked in the centre. Serve immediately.

BLUE CHEESE SOUFFLÉ

1 tablespoon butter, melted
30 g (1 oz) butter
30 g (¼ cup) plain (all-purpose)
   flour
250 ml (1 cup) milk
125 g (4½ oz) blue cheese,
   mashed
4 egg yolks
grated nutmeg
5 egg whites

SERVES 4

PREHEAT the oven to 200°C (400°F/Gas 6). Cut a strip of greaseproof paper long enough to fold around a 1.25 litre (5 cup) soufflé dish, then fold in half and tie around the dish so it sticks 2.5 cm (1 inch) above the top. Brush the inside of the dish and the collar with the melted butter and place the dish on a baking tray.

MELT the butter in a heavy-based saucepan and stir in the flour to make a roux. Cook, stirring, for 2 minutes over low heat without allowing the roux to brown. Remove from the heat and add the milk gradually, stirring after each addition until smooth. Return to the heat and bring to the boil. Simmer, stirring, for 3 minutes, then remove from the heat.

STIR the cheese into the sauce until it melts (it might separate but keep stirring—it will correct itself). Beat in the yolks, one at a time, beating well after each addition. Season with nutmeg, salt and pepper and pour into a large mixing bowl.

WHISK the egg whites in a clean dry bowl until they form soft peaks. Spoon a quarter of the egg white onto the soufflé mixture and quickly but lightly fold it in, to loosen the mixture. Lightly fold in the remaining egg white. Pour into the soufflé dish.

BAKE for 20–25 minutes, or until the soufflé is well risen and wobbles slightly when tapped. Test with a skewer through a crack in the side of the soufflé—the skewer should come out clean or slightly moist. If the skewer is slightly moist, by the time the soufflé makes it to the table it will be cooked in the centre. Serve immediately.

Cook the roux for a couple of minutes without browning, then turn off the heat before adding the milk gradually. Removing the saucepan from the heat before adding each ingredient prevents the sauce becoming lumpy.

MOUNTAIN CHEESES Each spring in the French Alps, herds of cows begin their annual transhumance from the winter lowlands to the *alpages,* the highland pastures. The farmers live in chalets while their herds eat the grass, herbs and flowers that will result in the rich, high-fat milk needed to produce cheeses such as reblochon and beaufort d'alpage, aged in cellars below their chalets.

CHEESE

FRANCE PROUDLY PRODUCES OVER 500 VARIETIES OF CHEESES, MANY OF THEM AMONG THE WORLD'S BEST, AND A REFLECTION OF THE STRENGTH OF REGIONAL TRADITIONS THAT HAD GENERAL DE GAULLE FAMOUSLY ASKING HOW ANYONE COULD GOVERN A COUNTRY WITH SO MANY CHEESES.

THE APPELLATION D'ORIGINE CONTRÔLÉE (AOC)

The AOC is granted to quality cheeses produced in a specified region following established production methods. AOC cheeses can be distinguished by a stamp and often by wording on the package such as *Fabrication traditionnelle au lait cru avec moulé à la louche* on AOC camembert.

CHEESEMAKERS

Fermier cheeses are farmhouse cheeses, using milk from the farmer's herd and traditional methods. *Artisanal* cheeses come from independent farmers using their own or others' milk. *Coopérative* cheeses are made at a dairy with milk coming from cooperative members. *Industriel* cheeses are produced in factories. Many *artisanal* and *fermier* cheesemakers have made traditional cheeses for generations, often in small quantities and sold just within their region. Only a few AOC or well-known cheeses reach a wider audience. Some cheese, such as camembert, is produced by *fermier, coopérative* and *industriel* methods with very different qualities.

MILK FOR CHEESE

French cheeses are made from cow's, goat's and sheep's milk, with ewe's milk being the strongest in flavour. Milk is pasteurized or *lait cru* (raw), which produces more complex flavours as the cheese develops. All *fermier* cheeses are made of *lait cru* and it is compulsory for some AOC cheeses.

CAMEMBERT is made at Isigny Ste Mère in Normandy using *industriel* methods but following AOC guidelines to the letter. First, a starter is added to the milk and left overnight. The milk is heated to no more than 37ºC, rennet added and the milk left to coagulate. Five portions of curds are ladled into perforated plastic moulds (*moulé à la louche*), with time between each 'pass' to evenly distribute the fat. The whey is

GOAT'S MILK CHEESES are produced all over France, with some of the most famous found in the Loire Valley, including the crottin de Chavignon, Provence and Corsica. Goat's cheeses were traditionally made seasonally, with the best cheeses produced in the spring from rich milk. Some are dusted with ash to encourage a mould to appear, while others are decorated with herbs or soaked in oil.

TYPES OF CHEESES

Cheeses can be categorized into families, and looking at the rind and the texture of the *pâte* (inside) of a cheese can help you determine its category and therefore roughly its taste.

FRESH CHEESE (fromage frais, chèvre frais) cheeses with no rind (because they haven't been ripened). A mild or slightly acidic taste and a high moisture content.

PÂTE FLEURIE (Camembert, Brie) soft cheeses with an edible white rind. These uncooked, unpressed (drained naturally) cheeses are high in moisture, causing white moulds to form a rind. A creamy, melting pâte and sometimes a mushroom taste.

PÂTE LAVÉE (Munster and Livarot) soft cheeses with washed rinds. These uncooked, unpressed high-moisture cheeses develop a cat's-fur mould when ripening, which is washed away in a process that encourages sticky orange bacteria to ripen the cheese from the outside in. They often have a smooth, elastic pâte, piquant taste and pungent aroma.

FROMAGES DE CHÈVRE goat's cheeses. These uncooked, unpressed cheeses have a slightly wrinkled rind and fresh taste when young, while older cheeses are more wrinkly, often with a blue mould (sometimes encouraged by dusting with ash) and a more intense, nutty, goat flavour.

PÂTE PERSILLÉE (Roquefort, Bleu d'Auvergne) blue cheeses. A penicillium is introduced into the cheeses, which in some cases, via airholes, spreads into blue veins. These uncooked, unpressed cheeses tend to have a sharp flavour and aroma.

PÂTE PRESSÉE (Cantal, Port-du-Salut) semi-hard cheeses with a supple rind that hardens with age. These uncooked cheeses are pressed so the dry cheese matures slowly to produce a well-developed, mellow taste. They are washed to seal the rind and moulds brushed off as the cheese ripens, or sealed in plastic or wax to stop the rind forming. The pâte varies from supple to hard if aged.

PÂTE CUITE (Beaufort, Emmental) hard mountain cheeses with a thick rind, depending on their age. These are cheeses whose curds have been finely cut, cooked and pressed and can be matured for a long time. They often have a fruity or nutty flavour and, with little moisture, a high fat content.

drained, then the cheeses removed from the moulds, salted and sprayed with mould and moved to drying rooms for two weeks while the white mould grows. Finally, the cheeses are wrapped in waxed paper and put in a wooden box to continue to age. There is up to four weeks of maturing (*affinage*) in the box, with many locals preferring the cheese when it is *moitié affiné* (half mature), with the heart not yet creamy.

PIPERADE

THIS TRADITIONAL BASQUE DISH IS A DELICIOUS MELDING OF RATATOUILLE AND EGGS. THE NAME IS DERIVED FROM '*PIPER*', MEANING RED PEPPER IN THE LOCAL DIALECT. THE EGGS CAN EITHER BE COOKED MORE LIKE AN OMELETTE OR SCRAMBLED TOGETHER AS DONE HERE.

2 tablespoons olive oil
1 large onion, thinly sliced
2 red capsicums (peppers), seeded
    and cut into batons
2 garlic cloves, crushed
750 g (1 lb 10 oz) tomatoes
pinch of cayenne pepper
8 eggs, lightly beaten
2 teaspoons butter
4 thin slices of ham, such as
    Bayonne

SERVES 4

HEAT the oil in a large heavy-based frying pan and cook the onion for 3 minutes, or until it has softened. Add the capsicum and garlic, cover and cook for 8 minutes to soften—stir frequently and don't allow it to brown.

SCORE a cross in the top of each tomato. Plunge into boiling water for 20 seconds, then drain and peel the skin away from the cross. Chop the tomatoes, discarding the cores. Spoon the chopped tomato and cayenne over the pepper, cover the pan and cook for a further 5 minutes.

UNCOVER the pan and increase the heat. Cook for 3 minutes or until the juices have evaporated, shaking the pan often. Season well with salt and pepper. Add the eggs and scramble into the mixture until they are cooked.

HEAT the butter in a small frying pan and fry the ham. Arrange on the piperade and serve at once.

Add the egg and scramble lightly into the piperade, remembering that it will continue to cook after it is removed from the heat.

OEUFS EN COCOTTE

1 tablespoon butter, melted
125 ml (1/2 cup) thick
    (double/heavy) cream
4 button mushrooms, finely
    chopped
40 g (1 1/2 oz) ham, finely chopped
40 g (1 1/2 oz) Gruyère cheese,
    finely chopped
4 eggs
1 tablespoon finely chopped herbs
    such as chervil, parsley, chives

SERVES 4

PREHEAT the oven to 200°C (400°F/Gas 6) and put a baking tray on the top shelf. Grease four ramekins with melted butter. Pour half the cream into the ramekins and then put a quarter of the mushrooms, ham and cheese into each. Break an egg into each ramekin. Mix the remaining cream with the herbs and pour over the top.

BAKE FOR 15–20 minutes on the hot baking tray, depending on how runny you like your eggs. Remove from the oven while still a little runny as the eggs will continue to cook. Season well and serve immediately with crusty toasted bread.

OEUFS EN COCOTTE

OEUFS EN CROUSTADE

A CROUSTADE IS A HOLLOWED-OUT PIECE OF BREAD THAT HAS BEEN FRIED OR BAKED TO MAKE A FIRM LITTLE CASE FOR FILLINGS. CROUSTADES PROVIDE THE PERFECT BASE FOR POACHED EGGS. FOR A NEATER FINISH, TRIM EACH EGG INTO A CIRCLE TO FIT THE HOLLOW.

CROUSTADES
1 stale unsliced loaf white bread
50 g (1³/₄ oz) butter, melted
1 garlic clove, crushed

HOLLANDAISE SAUCE
2 egg yolks
2 teaspoons lemon juice
90 g (3¹/₄ oz) unsalted butter, cut
   into cubes

4 eggs
1 teaspoon finely chopped parsley

SERVES 4

TO MAKE the croustades, preheat the oven to 180°C (350°F/Gas 4). Cut four 3 cm (1¹/₄ inch) thick slices from the bread and remove the crusts. Cut each piece of bread into a 9 cm (3¹/₂ inch) square, then use a 6.5 cm (2¹/₂ inch) round cutter to cut a circle in the centre of the bread, without cutting all the way through. Use a knife to scoop out the bread from the centre to form a hollow.

MIX TOGETHER the melted butter and garlic and brush all over the bread. Place on a baking tray and bake for 8 minutes, or until crisp and lightly golden. Keep warm.

TO MAKE the hollandaise sauce, put the egg yolks and lemon juice in a saucepan over very low heat. Whisk continuously, adding the butter piece by piece until the sauce thickens. Do not overheat or the eggs will scramble. Season with salt and pepper. The sauce should be of pouring consistency—if it is a little too thick, add 1–2 tablespoons of hot water to thin it a little.

(ALTERNATIVELY, put the eggs yolks, salt and pepper in a blender and mix together. Heat the lemon juice and butter together until boiling and then, with the motor running, pour onto the yolks in a steady stream.)

TO POACH the eggs, bring a pan of water to the boil. Crack an egg into a small bowl, reduce the heat and slide the egg into the simmering water. Poach for 3 minutes, then remove carefully with a slotted spoon and drain on paper towels. Poach the other three eggs. Trim the eggs of any straggly bits of white.

GENTLY PLACE an egg into each croustade. Pour over a little hollandaise sauce and sprinkle with parsley. Serve at once with extra hollandaise.

Use the freshest eggs you can find for poaching, so that the whites don't spread too much in the water. If you can't guarantee their freshness, add a little vinegar to the water to keep the whites together.

ONION TART

1 quantity tart pastry (page 278)
50 g (1³/₄ oz) butter
550 g (1 lb 4 oz) onions, finely
    sliced
2 teaspoons thyme leaves
3 eggs
280 ml (1¹/₄ cups) thick
    (double/heavy) cream
65 g (¹/₂ cup) grated Gruyère
    cheese
grated nutmeg

SERVES 6

PREHEAT the oven to 180°C (350°F/Gas 4). Line a 23 cm (9 inch) fluted loose-based tart tin with the pastry. Line the pastry shell with crumpled greaseproof paper and baking beads (use dried beans or rice if you don't have beads). Blind bake the pastry for 10 minutes, remove the paper and beads and bake for a further 3–5 minutes, or until the pastry is just cooked but still very pale.

MEANWHILE, melt the butter in a small frying pan and cook the onion, stirring, for 10–15 minutes or until tender and lightly browned. Add the thyme leaves and stir well. Leave to cool. Whisk together the eggs and cream and add the cheese. Season with salt, pepper and nutmeg.

SPREAD the onion into the pastry shell and pour the egg mixture over the top. Bake for 35–40 minutes, or until golden brown. Leave in the tin for 5 minutes before serving.

Cook the onion for the tart slowly to bring out the sweetness.

FLAMICHE

A SPECIALITY OF THE PICARDIE REGION, FLAMICHE IS MADE BOTH AS AN OPEN TART AND A CLOSED PIE. YOU WILL USUALLY COME ACROSS IT WITH A LEEK FILLING, AS HERE, BUT IT CAN ALSO BE MADE WITH ONION OR PUMPKIN.

FLAMICHE

1 quantity tart pastry (page 278)
500 g (1 lb 2 oz) leeks, white part
    only, finely sliced
50 g (1³/₄ oz) butter
175 g (6 oz) Maroilles (soft cheese),
    Livarot or Port-Salut, chopped
1 egg
1 egg yolk
60 ml (¹/₄ cup) thick (double/heavy)
    cream
1 egg, lightly beaten

SERVES 6

PREHEAT the oven to 180°C (350°F/Gas 4) and put a baking tray on the top shelf. Use ³/₄ of the pastry to line a 23 cm (9 inch) fluted loose-based tart tin.

COOK the leek for 10 minutes in boiling salted water, then drain. Heat the butter in a frying pan, add the leek and cook, stirring, for 5 minutes. Stir in the cheese. Tip into a bowl and add the egg, egg yolk and cream. Season and mix well.

POUR the filling into the pastry shell and smooth. Roll out the remaining pastry to cover the pie. Pinch the edges together and trim. Cut a hole in the centre and brush egg over the top. Bake for 35–40 minutes on the baking tray until browned. Leave in the tin for 5 minutes before serving.

QUICHE LORRAINE

TRADITIONALLY SERVED ON MAY DAY TO CELEBRATE THE START OF SPRING, QUICHE LORRAINE IS A REGIONAL DISH FROM NANCY IN LORRAINE AND IS MADE USING BACON, ANOTHER SPECIALITY OF THE AREA. THIS FOLLOWS THE ORIGINAL RECIPE, WHICH WAS MADE WITHOUT CHEESE.

1 quantity tart pastry (page 278)
25 g (1 oz) butter
300 g (10 1/2 oz) streaky bacon, diced
250 ml (1 cup) thick (double/heavy) cream
3 eggs
grated nutmeg

SERVES 8

PREHEAT the oven to 200°C (400°F/Gas 6). Line a 25 cm (10 inch) fluted loose-based tart tin with the pastry. Line the pastry shell with a crumpled piece of greaseproof paper and baking beads (use dried beans or rice). Blind bake the pastry for 10 minutes, remove the paper and beads and bake for a further 3–5 minutes, or until the pastry is just cooked but still very pale. Reduce the oven to 180°C (350°F/Gas 4).

MELT the butter in a small frying pan and cook the bacon until golden. Drain on paper towels.

MIX TOGETHER the cream and eggs and season with salt, pepper and nutmeg. Scatter the bacon into the pastry shell and then pour in the egg mixture. Bake for 30 minutes, or until the filling is set. Leave in the tin for 5 minutes before serving.

Blind bake and then fill the pastry on the oven shelf, so you don't need to worry about spillages.

BLUE CHEESE QUICHE

100 g (1 cup) walnuts
1 quantity tart pastry (page 278)
200 g (7 oz) blue cheese, mashed
80 ml (1/3 cup) milk
3 eggs
2 egg yolks
185 ml (3/4 cup) thick (double/heavy) cream

SERVES 8

PREHEAT the oven to 200°C (400°F/Gas 6). Toast the walnuts on a baking tray for 5 minutes, then chop. Line a 25 cm (10 inch) fluted loose-based tart tin with the pastry. Line the pastry shell with a crumpled piece of greaseproof paper and baking beads (use dried beans or rice). Blind bake the pastry for 10 minutes, remove the paper and beads and bake for a further 3–5 minutes, or until the pastry is just cooked but still very pale. Reduce the oven to 180°C (350°F/Gas 4).

MIX TOGETHER the blue cheese, milk, eggs, egg yolks and cream and season. Pour into the pastry shell and scatter with the walnuts. Bake for 25–30 minutes, or until the filling is just set. Leave in the tin for 5 minutes before serving.

BLUE CHEESE QUICHE

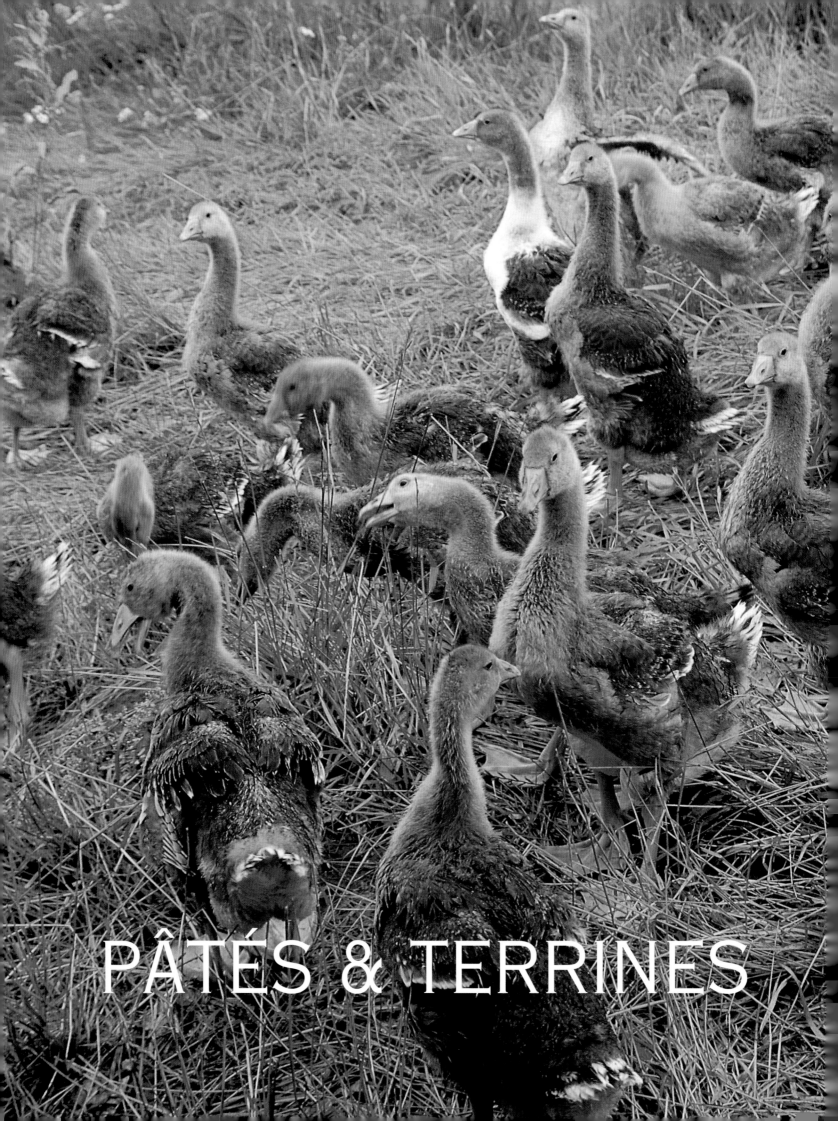

PÂTÉS & TERRINES

Gently fry the onion and garlic before adding the chicken livers and thyme. Once the livers have changed colour, add the brandy.

CHICKEN LIVER PÂTÉ

500 g (1 lb 2 oz) chicken livers
80 ml (1/3 cup) brandy
90 g (31/4 oz) unsalted butter
1 onion, finely chopped
1 garlic clove, crushed
1 teaspoon chopped thyme
60 ml (1/4 cup) thick (double/heavy)
  cream
4 slices white bread

SERVES 6

TRIM the chicken livers, cutting away any discoloured bits and veins. Rinse them, pat dry with paper towels and cut in half. Place in a small bowl with the brandy, cover and leave for a couple of hours. Drain the livers, reserving the brandy.

MELT half of the butter in a frying pan, add the onion and garlic and cook over low heat until the onion is soft and transparent. Add the livers and thyme and stir over moderate heat until the livers change colour. Add the reserved brandy and simmer for 2 minutes. Cool for 5 minutes.

PLACE the livers and liquid in a food processor and whiz until smooth. Add the remaining butter, chopped, and process again until smooth. (Alternatively, roughly mash the livers with a fork, then push them through a sieve and mix with the melted butter.) Pour in the cream and process until just incorporated.

SEASON the pâté and spoon into an earthenware dish or terrine, smoothing the surface. Cover and refrigerate until firm. If the pâté is to be kept for more than a day, chill it and then pour clarified butter over the surface to seal.

TO MAKE Melba toasts, preheat the grill (broiler) and cut the crusts off the bread. Toast the bread on both sides and then slice horizontally with a sharp serrated knife, to give eight pieces. Carefully toast the uncooked side of each slice and then cut it into two triangles. Serve with the pâté.

TERRINE DE CAMPAGNE

THIS IS THE DISH THAT YOU WILL FIND IN RESTAURANTS IF YOU ORDER *PÂTÉ MAISON*. IT IS OFTEN SERVED WITH PICKLED VEGETABLES AND COARSE COUNTRY BREAD. TERRINE DE CAMPAGNE FREEZES VERY WELL IF YOU HAVE SOME LEFTOVER OR WANT TO MAKE IT IN ADVANCE.

700 g (1 lb 9 oz) lean pork, cut into cubes
200 g (7 oz) pork belly, cut into strips
200 g (7 oz) chicken livers, trimmed
100 g (3^1/$_2$ oz) streaky bacon, chopped
1^1/$_2$ teaspoons sea salt
^{1}/$_2$ teaspoon black pepper
pinch of grated nutmeg
8 juniper berries, lightly crushed
3 tablespoons brandy
2 French shallots, finely chopped
1 large egg, lightly beaten
sprig of bay leaves
8 thinly sliced rashers streaky bacon

SERVES 8

PUT the lean pork, pork belly, chicken livers and chopped streaky bacon in a food processor and roughly chop into small dice (you will need to do this in two or three batches). Alternatively, finely dice the meat with a sharp knife.

PUT the diced meat in a large bowl and add the sea salt, pepper, nutmeg, juniper berries and brandy. Mix carefully and leave to marinate in the fridge for at least 6 hours or overnight.

PREHEAT the oven to 180°C (350°F/Gas 4). Lightly butter a 20 x 7 x 9 cm (8 x 2^3/$_4$ x 3^1/$_2$ inch) terrine or loaf tin. Add the shallots and egg to the marinated meat and carefully mix together.

PUT a sprig of bay leaves in the base of the terrine and then line with the rashers of bacon, leaving enough hanging over the sides to cover the top. Spoon the filling into the terrine and fold the ends of the bacon over the top. Cover the top with a layer of well-buttered greaseproof paper and then wrap the whole terrine in a layer of foil.

PLACE the terrine in a large baking dish and pour water into the baking dish to come halfway up the sides of the terrine. Bake in this bain-marie for 1^1/$_2$ hours, or until the pâté is shrinking away from the sides of the terrine.

LIFT the terrine out of the bain-marie and leave the pâté to cool, still wrapped in the paper and foil. Once cold, drain off the excess juices and refrigerate for up to a week. You may find that a little moisture has escaped from the pâté—this is quite normal and prevents it from drying out. Run a knife around the inside of the terrine to loosen the pâté and then turn out onto a board and serve in slices.

The free-range chicken and egg stall at a Lyon market.

PORK RILLETTES

OFTEN KNOWN AS *RILLETTES DE TOURS*, THIS SPECIALITY OF THE LOIRE VALLEY IS THE FRENCH VERSION OF POTTED MEAT. SPREAD ON TOAST OR BREAD AND SERVE WITH A GLASS OF WINE, OR STIR A SPOONFUL INTO SOUPS AND STEWS TO ADD FLAVOUR.

750 g (1 lb 10 oz) pork neck or
  belly, rind and bones removed
150 g (5^1/$_2$ oz) pork back fat
100 ml (3^1/$_2$ fl oz) dry white wine
3 juniper berries, lightly crushed
1 teaspoon sea salt
2 teaspoons dried thyme
^{1}/$_2$ teaspoon ground nutmeg
^{1}/$_4$ teaspoon ground allspice
pinch of ground cloves
1 large garlic clove, crushed

SERVES 8

PREHEAT the oven to 140°C (275°F/Gas 1). Cut the meat and fat into short strips and put in a casserole dish with the rest of the ingredients. Mix together thoroughly and cover with a lid. Bake for 4 hours, by which time the pork should be soft and surrounded by liquid fat.

TIP the meat and fat into a sieve placed over a bowl to collect the fat. Shred the warm meat with two forks. Season if necessary. Pack the meat into a 750 ml (3 cup) dish or terrine and leave until cold. Strain the hot fat through a sieve lined with damp muslin.

ONCE the pork is cold, pour the fat over it (you may need to melt the fat first, if it has solidified as it cooled). Cover and refrigerate for up to a week. Serve at room temperature.

PORK RILLETTES

DUCK RILLETTES

600 g (1 lb 5 oz) pork belly, rind
  and bones removed
800 g (1 lb 12 oz) duck legs
100 ml (3^1/$_2$ fl oz) dry white wine
1 teaspoon sea salt
^{1}/$_4$ teaspoon black pepper
^{1}/$_2$ teaspoon ground nutmeg
^{1}/$_4$ teaspoon ground allspice
1 large garlic clove, crushed

SERVES 8

PREHEAT the oven to 140°C (275°F/Gas 1). Cut the pork belly into small pieces and put in a casserole dish with the rest of the ingredients and 200 ml (7 fl oz) water. Mix together thoroughly and cover with a lid. Bake for 4 hours, by which time the meat should be soft and surrounded by liquid fat.

TIP the meat and fat into a sieve over a bowl to collect the fat. Remove the meat from the duck legs and shred all the warm meat with two forks. Season if necessary. Pack the meat into a 750 ml (3 cup) dish or terrine and leave until cold. Strain the hot fat through a sieve lined with damp muslin.

ONCE the meat is cold, pour the fat over it (you may need to melt the fat first, if it has solidified as it cooled). Cover and refrigerate for up to a week. Serve at room temperature.

Use two forks to shred the meat.

DUCK RILLETTES

SALMON TERRINE

IF YOU CAN FIND WILD SALMON IT WILL GIVE YOU A MUCH BETTER FLAVOUR THAN FARMED. A MILD SMOKED SALMON IS BETTER THAN A REALLY SMOKY ONE—SOME SMOKED SALMON VARIETIES CAN BE SO STRONG THEY MAKE THEIR PRESENCE FELT THROUGHOUT THE WHOLE TERRINE.

700 g (1 lb 9 oz) salmon fillet,
    skinned and all small bones
    removed
4 eggs
560 ml (2¼ cups) thick
    (double/heavy) cream
10 g (¼ oz) finely chopped chervil
250 g (9 oz) button mushrooms
1 teaspoon lemon juice
30 g (1 oz) butter
1 tablespoon grated onion
2 tablespoons white wine
10 large English spinach leaves
300 g (10½ oz) smoked salmon,
    thinly sliced

LEMON MAYONNAISE
1 tablespoon lemon juice
grated zest of 1 lemon
250 ml (1 cup) mayonnaise
    (page 286)

SERVES 8

PREHEAT the oven to 170°C (325°F/Gas 3). Purée the salmon fillet and eggs in a food processor until smooth. Push through a fine sieve into a glass bowl. (Alternatively, mash with a fork and push through a fine sieve.) Place over iced water and gradually mix in the cream. Stir in the chervil and season. Cover and leave in the fridge.

DICE the mushrooms and toss with the lemon juice to prevent discolouring. Melt the butter in a frying pan and cook the onion, stirring, for 2 minutes. Add the mushrooms and cook for 4 minutes. Add the wine and cook until it has evaporated. Season and remove from the heat.

DIP the spinach leaves in boiling water, then remove them carefully with a slotted spoon and lay them flat on paper towels.

BRUSH a 20 x 7 x 9 cm (8 x 2¾ x 3½ inch) terrine or loaf tin with oil and line the base with baking paper. Line the base and sides with the smoked salmon, leaving enough hanging over the sides to cover the top. Spoon in enough salmon mixture to half-fill the terrine. Lay half the spinach over the salmon, then spread with the mushrooms and another layer of spinach. Cover with the remaining salmon mixture, fold over the smoked salmon and cover with buttered baking paper.

PLACE the terrine in a large baking dish and pour water into the baking dish to come halfway up the side of the terrine. Bake in this bain-marie for 45–50 minutes, or until a skewer inserted into the terrine comes out clean. Leave for 5 minutes before unmoulding onto a serving plate. Peel off the baking paper, cover and chill the terrine.

TO MAKE the lemon mayonnaise, stir the lemon juice and zest through the mayonnaise and serve with slices of salmon terrine.

Line the terrine with smoked salmon, leaving the slices hanging over the sides. Once the terrine is filled, fold the smoked salmon over to cover the top.

VEGETABLE TERRINE WITH HERB SAUCE

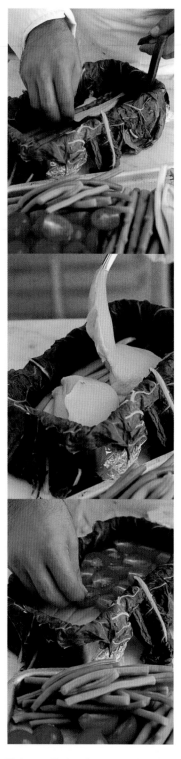

750 g (1 lb 10 oz) carrots, cut into
    chunks
8 large silverbeet (Swiss chard)
    leaves (or 16 smaller)
12 asparagus spears
2 small zucchini (courgettes)
16 green beans, topped and tailed
250 g (9 oz) crème fraîche
6 teaspoons powdered gelatine
16 cherry tomatoes, halved

HERB SAUCE
1 tablespoon finely chopped parsley
1 tablespoon finely chopped chervil
1 tablespoon finely shredded basil
grated zest of 1 small lemon
300 g (10^1/$_2$ oz) crème fraîche

SERVES 8

COOK the carrot in boiling water for 25 minutes
or until tender, then drain and cool. Dip the
silverbeet leaves in boiling water, then remove
carefully with a slotted spoon and lay flat on
paper towels.

LIGHTLY OIL a 20 x 7 x 9 cm (8 x 2^3/$_4$ x 3^1/$_2$ inch)
terrine or loaf tin. Line with a layer of plastic wrap,
leaving enough hanging over the sides to cover
the top. Then line the tin with the silverbeet
leaves, make sure there are no gaps, and leaving
enough hanging over the sides to cover the top.

TRIM the asparagus spears at the thicker ends
so they fit the length of the terrine. Slice each
zucchini in half lengthways, then each half into
four lengthways. Steam the asparagus, zucchini
and beans for 6 minutes, or until tender to the
point of a knife. Drain and refresh in cold water so
they keep their colour. Pat dry with paper towels.

PURÉE the carrots with the crème fraîche in a
food processor, or mash and push through a
sieve, and season well. Put 2 tablespoons water
in a small bowl and sprinkle with the gelatine.
Leave for 5 minutes until spongy, then put the
bowl over a pan of simmering water until melted.
Add to the carrot purée and mix well.

SPOON a quarter of the carrot purée into the
terrine, then arrange six asparagus spears on top,
all pointing in the same direction. Arrange the
zucchini on top, in one flat layer. Smooth over
another quarter of carrot purée, then a layer of
tomatoes, cut sides upwards. Spoon over another
layer of carrot purée and then the beans. Arrange
the rest of the asparagus on top and finally the
remaining carrot purée. Fold over the overhanging
silverbeet leaves and plastic wrap to cover the
top. Leave in the fridge overnight. Unmould onto a
plate, peel off the plastic wrap and cut into slices.

TO MAKE the herb sauce, fold the herbs and
lemon zest into the crème fraîche and season
well. Serve with the vegetable terrine.

Take a little time to trim the
vegetables to the same size and
arrange the layers as neatly and
evenly as you can.

PÂTÉ EN CROÛTE

THE WORD 'PÂTÉ', MEANING CRUST, WAS TRADITIONALLY ONLY USED WHEN REFERRING TO THIS DISH.

THESE DAYS, THE WORDS PÂTÉ AND TERRINE ARE USED INTERCHANGEABLY AND PÂTÉ IS SYNONYMOUS

WITH ALL KINDS OF MEAT AND SEAFOOD PASTES, NOT JUST THOSE WITH A PASTRY CRUST.

600 g (1 lb 5 oz) veal fillet, finely
    diced
250 g (9 oz) lean pork, finely diced
200 g (7 oz) streaky bacon, finely
    diced
large pinch of ground cloves
large pinch of allspice
finely grated zest of 1 lemon
2 tablespoons brandy
2 bay leaves
2 teaspoons butter
1 large garlic clove, crushed
1 onion, finely chopped
200 g (7 oz) wild or chestnut
    mushrooms, finely chopped
3 tablespoons finely chopped
    parsley
1 quantity puff pastry (page 281)
1 egg, lightly beaten

SERVES 8

MIX TOGETHER the veal, pork, streaky bacon, cloves, allspice, lemon zest and brandy. Stir well, tuck the bay leaves into the mixture, then cover and leave to marinate in the fridge for at least 6 hours or preferably overnight.

MELT the butter in a frying pan and add the garlic and onion. Cook over low heat for 10 minutes, then add the mushrooms and cook for a further 10 minutes, until they are softened and the liquid from the mushrooms has evaporated. Stir in the parsley and leave to cool.

REMOVE the bay leaves from the marinated meat. Add the cold mushroom mixture to the raw meat, season well and mix together thoroughly.

PREHEAT the oven to 200°C (400°F/Gas 6). Roll out the pastry on a lightly floured surface into a 38 cm (15 inch) square, trim the edges and keep for decoration. Pile the meat mixture onto the middle of the pastry, shaping it into a rectangle about 30 cm (12 inches) long. Brush the edges of the pastry with a little beaten egg. Fold the pastry over the meat as if you were wrapping a parcel. Place on a baking tray, seam side down.

DECORATE the parcel with shapes cut from the pastry scraps and brush all over with beaten egg. Cook on the middle shelf of the oven for 15 minutes, then reduce the temperature to 180°C (350°F/Gas 4) and cook for 1–1¼ hours, or until the filling is cooked and the pastry golden brown. Cool completely before serving in slices with pickles.

Pâté for sale at a Provence market.

SEAFOOD

POACHED SEAFOOD WITH HERB AÏOLI

THE BEST WAY TO APPROACH THIS RECIPE IS AS A GUIDE—AS WITH ALL SEAFOOD COOKING, YOU

SHOULD ALWAYS ASK YOUR FISHMONGER'S ADVICE AS TO WHAT'S THE BEST CATCH THAT DAY. DON'T

FORGET TO PROVIDE FINGERBOWLS.

2 raw lobster tails
12 mussels
250 g (9 oz) scallops on their shells
500 g (1 lb 2 oz) prawns (shrimp)
250 ml (1 cup) dry white wine
250 ml (1 cup) fish stock
pinch of saffron threads
1 bay leaf
4 black peppercorns
4 x 50 g (1¾ oz) salmon fillets

HERB AÏOLI
4 egg yolks
4 garlic cloves, crushed
1 tablespoon chopped basil
4 tablespoons chopped flat-leaf
    (Italian) parsley
1 tablespoon lemon juice
200 ml (7 fl oz) olive oil

lemon wedges

SERVES 4

REMOVE the lobster meat from the tail by cutting down each side of the underside with scissors and peeling back the middle piece of shell. Scrub the mussels and remove their beards, discarding any that are open and don't close when tapped on the work surface. Remove the scallops from their shells and pull away the white muscle and digestive tract around each one, leaving the roes intact. Clean the scallop shells and keep them for serving. Peel and devein the prawns, leaving the tails intact, and butterfly them by cutting them open down the backs.

TO MAKE the herb aïoli, put the egg yolks, garlic, basil, parsley and lemon juice in a mortar and pestle or food processor and pound or mix until light and creamy. Add the oil, drop by drop from the tip of a teaspoon, pounding constantly until the mixture begins to thicken, then add the oil in a very thin stream. (If you're using a processor, pour in the oil in a thin stream with the motor running.)

PUT the wine, stock, saffron, bay leaf and peppercorns in a frying pan and bring to a very slow simmer. Add the lobster and poach for 5 minutes then remove, cover and keep warm.

POACH the remaining seafood in batches: the mussels and scallops will take about 2 minutes to cook and open (discard any mussels that have not opened after this time). The prawns will take 3 minutes and the salmon a little longer, depending on the thickness. (Keep the poaching liquid to use as soup stock.) Cut the lobster into thick medallions, put the scallops back on their shells and arrange the seafood on a large platter with the aïoli in a bowl in the centre. Serve with lemon wedges.

Cut down each side of the underside of the lobster tail and peel back the shell.

A busy Provence port.

CRAB SOUFFLÉS

1 tablespoon butter, melted
2 cloves
1/4 small onion
1 bay leaf
6 black peppercorns
250 ml (1 cup) milk
1 tablespoon butter
1 French shallot, finely chopped
15 g (1/2 oz) plain (all-purpose) flour
3 egg yolks
250 g (9 oz) cooked crab meat
pinch of cayenne pepper
5 egg whites

SERVES 6

PREHEAT the oven to 200°C (400°F/Gas 6). Brush six 125 ml (1/2 cup) ramekins with the melted butter.

PRESS the cloves into the onion, then put in a small saucepan with the bay leaf, peppercorns and milk. Gently bring to the boil, then remove from the heat and leave to infuse for 10 minutes. Strain the milk.

MELT the butter in a heavy-based saucepan, add the shallot and cook, stirring, for 3 minutes until softened but not browned. Stir in the flour to make a roux and cook, stirring, for 3 minutes over low heat without allowing the roux to brown.

REMOVE from the heat and add the infused milk gradually, stirring after each addition until smooth. Return to the heat and simmer for 3 minutes, stirring continuously. Beat in the egg yolks, one at a time, beating well after each addition. Add the crab meat and stir over the heat until the mixture is hot and thickens again (do not let it boil). Pour into a large heatproof bowl, then add the cayenne and season well.

WHISK the egg whites in a clean dry bowl until they form soft peaks. Spoon a quarter of the egg white onto the soufflé mixture and quickly but lightly fold it in, to loosen the mixture. Lightly fold in the remaining egg white. Pour into the ramekins and then run your thumb around the inside rim of each ramekin. This ridge helps the soufflés to rise evenly without sticking.

PUT the ramekins on a baking tray and bake for 12–15 minutes, or until the soufflés are well risen and wobble slightly when tapped. Test with a skewer through a crack in the side of a soufflé— the skewer should come out clean or slightly moist. If the skewer is slightly moist, by the time the soufflés make it to the table they will be cooked in the centre. Serve immediately.

Fold a quarter of the egg white into the soufflé mixture to loosen it up before you add the rest.

Unloading the catch in Marseille.

The Quai des Belges, Marseille.

COQUILLES SAINT JACQUES MORNAY

SCALLOPS IN FRANCE ARE NAMED AFTER SAINT JAMES. THEIR SHELLS WERE ONCE WORN BY PILGRIMS WHO FOUND THEM AS THEY WALKED ALONG THE SPANISH COAST ON THEIR PILGRIMAGE TO A CATHEDRAL IN SPAIN DEDICATED TO THE SAINT.

Poach the scallops in court bouillon first, so that they are thoroughly cooked before grilling (broiling). The heat of the grill (broiler) alone isn't enough to cook them.

COURT BOUILLON
250 ml (1 cup) white wine
1 onion, sliced
1 carrot, sliced
1 bay leaf
4 black peppercorns

24 scallops on their shells
50 g (1¾ oz) butter
3 French shallots, finely chopped
3 tablespoons plain (all-purpose) flour
410 ml (1⅔ cups) milk
130 g (1 cup) grated Gruyère cheese

SERVES 6

TO MAKE the court bouillon, put the wine, onion, carrot, bay leaf, peppercorns and 500 ml (2 cups) water into a deep frying pan, bring to the boil and simmer for 20 minutes. Strain the court bouillon and return to the clean frying pan.

REMOVE the scallops from their shells and pull away the white muscle and digestive tract from each one, leaving the roes intact. Clean the shells and keep for serving.

BRING the court bouillon to a gentle simmer, add the scallops and poach over low heat for 2 minutes. Remove the scallops from the court bouillon, drain and return to their shells. Pour away the court bouillon.

MELT the butter in a heavy-based saucepan, add the shallot and cook, stirring, for 3 minutes. Stir in the flour to make a roux and cook, stirring, for 3 minutes over low heat without allowing the roux to brown.

REMOVE from the heat and add the milk gradually, stirring after each addition until smooth. Return to the heat and simmer, stirring, for about 3 minutes, until the sauce has thickened. Remove from the heat and stir in the cheese until melted. Season with salt and pepper. Preheat the grill (broiler). Spoon the sauce over the scallops and place under the grill until golden brown. Serve immediately.

GARLIC PRAWNS

24 large prawns (shrimp)
6 garlic cloves, crushed
1–2 small red chillies, very finely
    chopped
250 ml (1 cup) olive oil
60 g (2¼ oz) butter
2 tablespoons chopped parsley

SERVES 4

PEEL and devein the prawns, leaving the tails intact. Preheat the oven to 220°C (425°F/Gas 7). Sprinkle the garlic and chilli into four cast iron or gratin dishes. Divide the oil and butter among the dishes.

PUT the dishes on a baking tray in the oven and heat for about 6 minutes, or until the butter has melted.

DIVIDE the prawns among the dishes (put them in carefully, without splashing yourself with hot oil) and bake for about 7 minutes, or until the prawns are pink and tender. Sprinkle with parsley and serve immediately with crusty bread.

SNAILS WITH GARLIC BUTTER

THERE ARE MANY VARIETIES OF EDIBLE SNAILS, WITH THE MOST COMMON BEING *PETITS GRIS* OR THE SLIGHTLY LARGER *ESCARGOTS DE BOURGOGNE*, ALSO KNOWN AS THE ROMAN SNAIL. CANNED SNAILS ARE SOLD ALONG WITH THEIR SHELLS AND ARE EASIER TO USE THAN FRESH ONES.

Simmer the snails and then leave to cool in the poaching liquid.

250 ml (1 cup) white wine
250 ml (1 cup) chicken stock
3 sprigs of tarragon
24 canned snails, well drained
24 snail shells
2 garlic cloves, crushed
2 tablespoons finely chopped basil
    leaves
2 tablespoons finely chopped
    parsley
2 tablespoons finely chopped
    tarragon leaves
150 g (5½ oz) butter, at room
    temperature

SERVES 4

PUT the wine, stock, tarragon and 125 ml (½ cup) water in a small saucepan and boil for 2 minutes. Add the snails and simmer for 7 minutes. Remove from the heat and leave to cool in the poaching liquid. Drain and place a snail in each shell. Preheat the oven to 200°C (400°F/Gas 6).

MIX TOGETHER the garlic, basil, parsley and tarragon Mix in the butter and season well.

PUT a little garlic butter into each shell and arrange them on a snail plate or baking tray covered with a layer of rock salt. Bake for 7–8 minutes, or until the butter melts and the snails are heated through. Serve immediately with crusty bread to mop up the garlic butter.

SNAILS WITH GARLIC BUTTER

Leaving the skin on the fish is traditional as originally whole fish would have been used for this dish. The skin also helps the pieces hold together while the soup is cooking.

Fishermen selling their morning's catch on the Quai des Belges, in the old port of Marseille.

BOUILLABAISSE

BOUILLABAISSE IS THE MOST FAMOUS FRENCH FISH SOUP AND IS ASSOCIATED WITH THE SOUTH OF THE COUNTRY, PARTICULARLY MARSEILLE. AS A FISHERMAN'S MEAL IT IS OFTEN MADE WITH WHOLE FISH, ESPECIALLY *RASCASSE* (SCORPION FISH). USING FILLETS IS MUCH SIMPLER.

ROUILLE
1 small red capsicum (pepper)
1 slice white bread, crusts removed
1 red chilli
2 garlic cloves
1 egg yolk
80 ml (1/3 cup) olive oil

SOUP
18 mussels
1.5 kg (3 lb 5 oz) firm white fish
    fillets such as red mullet, bass,
    snapper, monkfish, rascasse,
    John Dory or eel, skin on
2 tablespoons oil
1 fennel bulb, thinly sliced
1 onion, chopped
750 g (1 lb 10 oz) ripe tomatoes
1.25 litres (5 cups) fish stock or
    water
pinch of saffron threads
bouquet garni
5 cm (2 inch) piece of orange zest

SERVES 6

TO MAKE the rouille, preheat the grill (broiler). Cut the capsicum in half, remove the seeds and membrane and place, skin side up, under the hot grill until the skin blackens and blisters. Leave to cool before peeling. Roughly chop the capsicum.

SOAK the bread in 3 tablespoons water, then squeeze dry with your hands. Put the capsicum, chilli, bread, garlic and egg yolk in a mortar and pestle or food processor and pound or mix together. Gradually add the oil in a thin stream, pounding or mixing until the rouille is smooth and has the texture of thick mayonnaise. Cover and refrigerate the rouille until needed.

TO MAKE the soup, scrub the mussels and remove their beards. Discard any mussels that are already open and don't close when tapped on the work surface. Cut the fish into bite-sized pieces.

HEAT the oil in a large saucepan and cook the fennel and onion over medium heat for 5 minutes, or until golden.

SCORE a cross in the top of each tomato. Plunge into boiling water for 20 seconds, then drain and peel the skin away from the cross. Chop the tomatoes, discarding the cores. Add to the pan and cook for 3 minutes. Stir in the stock, saffron, bouquet garni and orange zest, bring to the boil and boil for 10 minutes. Remove the bouquet garni and either push the soup through a sieve or purée in a blender. Return to the cleaned pan, season well and bring back to the boil.

REDUCE the heat to simmer and add the fish and mussels. Cook for 5 minutes or until the fish is tender and the mussels have opened. Throw out any mussels that haven't opened in this time. Serve the soup with rouille and bread. Or lift out the fish and mussels and serve separately.

LOBSTER THERMIDOR

LOBSTER THERMIDOR WAS CREATED FOR THE FIRST NIGHT CELEBRATIONS OF A PLAY CALLED 'THERMIDOR' IN PARIS IN 1894. TRADITIONALLY THE LOBSTER IS CUT IN HALF WHILE ALIVE, BUT FREEZING IT FIRST IS MORE HUMANE.

2 live lobsters
250 ml (1 cup) fish stock
2 tablespoons white wine
2 French shallots, finely chopped
2 teaspoons chopped chervil
2 teaspoons chopped tarragon
110 g (4 oz) butter
2 tablespoons plain (all-purpose) flour
1 teaspoon dry mustard
250 ml (1 cup) milk
65 g (2/3 cup) grated Parmesan cheese

SERVES 4

PUT the lobsters in the freezer an hour before you want to cook them. Bring a large pan of water to the boil, drop in the lobsters and cook for 10 minutes. Drain and cool slightly before cutting off the heads. Cut the lobster tails in half lengthways. Use a spoon to ease the lobster meat out of the shells and cut it into bite-sized pieces. Rinse the shells, pat dry and keep for serving.

PUT the stock, wine, shallot, chervil and tarragon into a small saucepan. Boil until reduced by half and then strain.

MELT 60 g (2¹/4 oz) of the butter in a heavy-based saucepan and stir in the flour and mustard to make a roux. Cook, stirring, for 2 minutes over low heat without allowing the roux to brown.

REMOVE from the heat and add the milk and the reserved stock mixture gradually, stirring after each addition until smooth. Return to the heat and stir constantly until the sauce boils and thickens. Simmer, stirring occasionally, for 3 minutes. Stir in half the Parmesan. Season with salt and pepper.

HEAT the remaining butter in a frying pan and fry the lobster over moderate heat for 2 minutes until lightly browned—take care not to overcook. Preheat the grill (broiler).

DIVIDE HALF the sauce among the lobster shells, top with the lobster meat and then finish with the remaining sauce. Sprinkle with the remaining Parmesan and place under the grill until golden brown and bubbling. Serve immediately.

Fry the lobster in butter until it is lightly browned, but take care not to overcook or it will toughen. Spoon the lobster and sauce into the cleaned shells for serving.

LOBSTER A L'AMÉRICAINE

4 live lobsters
4 tablespoons olive oil
1 onion, finely chopped
4 French shallots, finely chopped
1 carrot, finely chopped
1 celery stalk, finely chopped
1 garlic clove, crushed
500 g (1 lb 2 oz) ripe tomatoes
2 tablespoons tomato paste (purée)
125 ml (^{1}/$_2$ cup) white wine
2 tablespoons brandy
250 ml (1 cup) fish stock
bouquet garni
60 g (2^1/$_4$ oz) butter, softened
3 tablespoons chopped parsley

SERVES 4

Carefully remove the flesh from the lobster tails, by cutting away the underside of the shells. Cook the tails by simmering on top of the sauce. To finish off, stir the lobster roe and liver into the sauce for a rich flavour.

PUT the lobsters in the freezer an hour before you want to use them. Cut off the lobster heads and remove the claws. Heat the oil in a large frying pan and cook the lobster heads, tails and claws in batches over moderate heat until the lobster turns bright red and the flesh begins to shrink away from the shell.

ALLOW TO cool slightly before cutting the lobster heads in half and scraping out the red coral and the yellowy livers. Keep these to add flavour to the sauce.

CUT DOWN each side of the underside of the tail, then remove the centre piece of shell and carefully remove the meat from the tail.

ADD the onion and shallot to the saucepan with the lobster claws and head shells. Cook over moderate heat for 3 minutes, or until golden, then add the carrot, celery and garlic and cook for 5 minutes, or until soft.

SCORE a cross in the top of each tomato. Plunge into boiling water for 20 seconds, then drain and peel the skin away from the cross. Chop the tomatoes, discarding the cores. Add the tomato, tomato purée, wine, brandy, fish stock and bouquet garni to the pan and bring to the boil.

ARRANGE the meat from the lobster tails on top of the sauce, cover and simmer for 5 minutes, or until the lobster is cooked.

REMOVE the tail meat, heads and claws from the sauce, cover and keep warm. Continue cooking the sauce until it has reduced by half.

MIX the reserved coral and liver with the softened butter and stir this into the sauce with the parsley. Season with salt and pepper and remove the bouquet garni. Slice the tail meat into medallions and divide among four plates. Spoon the sauce over the lobster and decorate with the claws to serve if you like.

MOULES MARINIÈRE

GROWN ALL ALONG THE COAST OF FRANCE ON WOODEN POSTS, MUSSELS ARE REGIONAL TO MANY AREAS BUT ARE PARTICULARLY ASSOCIATED WITH BRITTANY, NORMANDY AND THE NORTHEAST. THIS IS ONE OF THE SIMPLEST WAYS TO SERVE THEM.

2 kg (4 lb 8 oz) mussels
40 g (1 1/2 oz) butter
1 large onion, chopped
1/2 celery stalk, chopped
2 garlic cloves, crushed
410 ml (1 2/3 cups) white wine
1 bay leaf
2 sprigs of thyme
185 ml (3/4 cup) thick
   (double/heavy) cream
2 tablespoons chopped parsley

SERVES 4

SCRUB the mussels and remove their beards. Discard any that are open already and don't close when tapped on the work surface. Melt the butter in a large saucepan and cook the onion, celery and garlic, stirring occasionally, over moderate heat until the onion is softened but not browned.

ADD the wine, bay leaf and thyme to the saucepan and bring to the boil. Add the mussels, cover the pan tightly and simmer over low heat for 2–3 minutes, shaking the pan occasionally. Use tongs to lift out the mussels as they open, putting them into a warm dish. Throw away any mussels that haven't opened after 3 minutes.

STRAIN the liquid through a fine sieve into a clean saucepan, leaving behind any grit or sand. Bring to the boil and boil for 2 minutes. Add the cream and reheat the sauce without boiling. Season well. Serve the mussels in individual bowls with the liquid poured over. Sprinkle with the parsley and serve with plenty of bread.

Wash the mussels, taking care to discard any that are already open and don't close when tapped.

GRILLED SARDINES

8 sardines
2 tablespoons olive oil
3 tablespoons lemon juice
1/2 lemon, halved and thinly sliced
lemon wedges

SERVES 4

SLIT the sardines along their bellies and remove the guts. Rinse well and pat dry. Use scissors to cut out the gills.

MIX TOGETHER the oil and lemon juice and season generously with salt and black pepper. Brush the inside and outside of each fish with the oil, then place a few lemon slices into each cavity.

PUT the sardines onto a preheated chargrill (griddle) and cook, basting frequently with the remaining oil, for about 2–3 minutes each side until cooked through. They can also be cooked under a very hot grill (broiler). Serve with lemon wedges.

GRILLED SARDINES

MOULES MARINIÈRE AND GRILLED SARDINES

LANGOUSTINES AU CURRIE

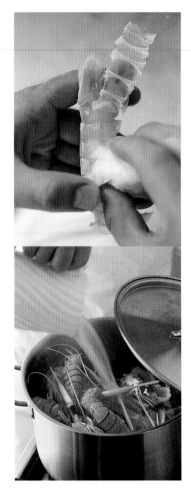

24 langoustines (Dublin Bay
  prawns)
25 g (1 oz) butter
1 teaspoon oil
1 tablespoon whisky

SAUCE
10 g (¼ oz) butter
1 tablespoon whisky
250 ml (1 cup) chicken stock
1 teaspoon curry powder
250 ml (1 cup) thick (double/heavy)
  cream

SERVES 4

TWIST the heads off the langoustines and peel, by cutting down both sides of the underside of the tail and pulling back the flap. Leave the last section of shell and tail attached. Keep the shells and heads.

TO MAKE the sauce, heat the butter in a saucepan, add the langoustine heads and shells and cook for 4 minutes. Add the whisky, chicken stock, curry powder and 60 ml (¼ cup) water and allow to boil until the sauce has reduced by half. Stir in the cream and keep boiling until the sauce has reduced by a third. Season and then strain.

TO COOK the langoustines, heat the butter and oil in a large frying pan, add the langoustines and cook for 3 minutes on each side. Add the whisky and flambé by lighting the pan with your gas flame or a match (stand well back when you do this and keep a pan lid handy for emergencies). The flames will last a short time. Put the langoustines on a plate and pour the sauce over the top.

Peel the langoustines, leaving the tails attached. Use the trimmings to add flavour to the sauce.

SOLE MEUNIÈRE

THIS CLASSIC RECIPE, SERVED IN SOME OF THE WORLD'S TOP RESTAURANTS, IS ACTUALLY A QUICK AND EASY STAPLE SUPPER IN FRANCE. MEUNIÈRE MEANS 'MILLERS' STYLE', PROBABLY REFERRING TO THE FLOUR FOR DUSTING. YOU CAN USE SOLE FILLETS IF YOU PREFER.

4 sole, gutted and dark skin
  removed (or use sole fillets)
3 tablespoons plain (all-purpose)
  flour
200 g (7 oz) clarified butter
2 tablespoons lemon juice
4 tablespoons chopped parsley
lemon wedges

SERVES 4

PAT the fish dry with paper towels, removing the heads if you prefer, and then dust lightly with the flour and season. Heat 150 g (5½ oz) of the butter in a frying pan large enough to fit all four fish, or use half the butter and cook the fish in two batches.

PUT the fish in the pan, skin side up, and cook for 4 minutes on each side or until golden. Lift the fish out onto warm plates and drizzle with the lemon juice and parsley. Add the remaining butter to the pan and heat until it browns to make a *beurre noisette*. Pour over the fish (it will foam as it mixes with the lemon juice) and serve with lemon wedges.

SOLE MEUNIÈRE

MARSEILLES OLD PORT is still a thriving fishing port, even though the main fish market has now moved undercover. Fishing here is very much a local and family industry and '*Pêche le nuit, vendu le matin*' (fish the night, sell in the morning) is the saying—though in reality the men go out in the early morning, not all night. The fishing boats arrive back at the Quay des Belges at about ten in the morning, when their

SEAFOOD

BORDERED BY WATER ON THREE SIDES, THE CHOICE OF

SEAFOOD AVAILABLE IN FRANCE IS PROBABLY UNSURPASSABLE,

AND THE FRENCH CERTAINLY KNOW HOW TO EAT IT—THIS IS A

COUNTRY FAMOUS FOR ITS WONDERFUL FISH DISHES.

The seafood comes from the Mediterranean to the south, the Bay of Biscay and the Atlantic to the west and the English Channel to the northwest, as well as freshwater fish from rivers and lakes. What is not available in home waters is snapped up elsewhere, with long-distance trawlers fishing as far away as the waters of Newfoundland and Iceland.

FISH MARKETS
The fishing fleets bring their catch into *criées,* or wholesale markets, where the seafood is auctioned early in the morning and then distributed to the towns and cities before daybreak. The most important of these markets is at the channel port of Boulogne, which services Paris, and also the fishing ports of Brittany and Normandy. Some of the daily catch may also be sold on the quayside, where fishermen bring their boats alongside and sell fish that are still alive from trays running with sea water. Away from the coast, *poissonneries* and supermarkets sell fish.

REGIONAL SPECIALITIES
In the Northwest, oysters, scallops, Dublin Bay prawns, clams and whelks can all be found on Brittany and Normandy's *plateau de fruits de mer,* riches from an area that has some of France's most important fishing ports.

catch is offloaded, still wriggling, into blue trays. Usually a family member sells the catch while the fishermen tidy up their boats and mend nets. As well as individual fish, mixtures of small fish are sold for frying and bonier fish for soup. The seafood, including octopus, is carried away live in plastic bags, though each stall also has a knife and chopping block, and fish can be gutted and filleted before being sold.

Brittany fleets fish for sardines and tuna, and the area also claims *lobster à l'américaine* as its own, while Normandy is famous for its *moules marinière,* stewy *marmite dieppoise* and its Dover sole, cooked as *sole normande*.

The centre of the fishing industry in the North is Boulogne, which has wonderful local sole and mussels, as well as fishing boats bringing in catches from the Mediterranean to the Atlantic. Inland, freshwater trout, prepared '*au bleu*', is a speciality of Alsace-Lorraine. In the Southwest there is Atlantic tuna from the Basque ports and oysters from Bordeaux.

Sardines and anchovies are a southern favourite from Languedoc-Roussillon on the Spanish border, while Provence's Mediterranean catch, from rascasse, chapon, mullet, conger eel, sea bass to bream, is transformed into wonderful dishes such as *bouillabaisse* and *bourride*.

SOLE NORMANDE

12 prawns (shrimp)
500 ml (2 cups) dry white wine
12 oysters, shucked
12 small button mushrooms
4 sole fillets
250 ml (1 cup) cream
1 truffle, thinly sliced
1 tablespoon chopped parsley

SERVES 4

PEEL and devein the prawns. Put the wine in a deep frying pan and bring to the boil. Add the oysters to the wine and poach for 2–3 minutes, then lift out with a slotted spoon, drain and keep warm. Poach the prawns in the wine for 3 minutes, or until pink and cooked through. Lift out and keep warm. Poach the mushrooms for 5 minutes, then lift out and keep warm. Add the sole fillets to the poaching liquid and cook for 5 minutes, or until cooked through. Lift out onto a serving dish, cover and keep warm.

ADD the cream to the poaching liquid and bring to the boil. Boil until the sauce has reduced by half and thickened enough to coat the back of a spoon. Season with salt and pepper.

PUT a sole fillet on each plate and scatter with the prawns, oysters and mushrooms, then pour the sauce over the top. Sprinkle with the sliced truffle and parsley and serve immediately.

Make a couple of slashes in the thickest part of the mullet so they cook quickly and evenly and the baste runs through the flesh.

GRILLED RED MULLET WITH HERB SAUCE

4 x 200 g (7 oz) red mullet
3 tablespoons lemon juice
3 tablespoons olive oil

HERB SAUCE
100 g (3¹/₂ oz) English spinach
  leaves
3 tablespoons olive oil
1 tablespoon white wine vinegar
1 tablespoon chopped parsley
1 tablespoon chopped chives
1 tablespoon chopped chervil
1 tablespoon finely chopped capers
2 anchovy fillets, finely chopped
1 hard-boiled egg, finely chopped

SERVES 4

PREHEAT a chargrill (griddle) or barbecue. Make a couple of deep slashes in the thickest part of each fish. Pat the fish dry and sprinkle inside and out with salt and pepper. Drizzle with a little lemon juice and olive oil and cook on the chargrill or barbecue for 4–5 minutes each side, or until the fish flakes when tested with the tip of a knife. Baste with the lemon juice and oil during cooking.

TO MAKE the sauce, wash the spinach and put it in a large saucepan with just the water clinging to the leaves. Cover the pan and steam the spinach for 2 minutes, or until just wilted. Drain, cool and squeeze with your hands to get rid of the excess liquid. Finely chop. Mix with the oil, vinegar, herbs, capers, anchovy and egg in a food processor or pestle and mortar. Spoon the sauce onto a plate and place the fish on top to serve.

GRILLED RED MULLET WITH
HERB SAUCE

BAKED TROUT WITH FENNEL AND CAPERS

PURISTS LIKE THEIR TROUT COOKED WITH THE MINIMUM OF FUSS, PERHAPS DRESSED WITH A LITTLE BUTTER AND LEMON. THE FENNEL AND CAPERS, HOWEVER, COMPLEMENT THE TROUT PERFECTLY, THEIR FLAVOUR PERMEATING THE DELICATE FLESH OF THE FISH DURING BAKING.

2 fennel bulbs, with fronds
1 leek, white part only, thickly sliced
1 large carrot, cut into batons
2 tablespoons olive oil
2 tablespoons capers, rinsed and
  patted dry
1 French shallot, finely chopped
1 x 1.3 kg (3 lb) brown or rainbow
  trout, or 4 x 300 g (10^1/$_2$ oz)
  trout, gutted and fins removed
1 or 2 bay leaves
25 g (1 oz) butter, cut into 4 cubes
4 slices lemon
185 ml (^{3}/$_4$ cup) fish stock
60 ml (^{1}/$_4$ cup) dry vermouth
2 tablespoons thick (double/heavy)
  cream
2 tablespoons chopped chervil

SERVES 4

PREHEAT the oven to 200°C (400°F/Gas 6). Cut off the fronds from the fennel bulbs and finely chop them. Thinly slice the bulbs and place in a roasting tin with the leek and carrot. Drizzle a tablespoon of olive oil over the vegetables, add salt and pepper and then toss well to coat them in the oil and seasoning. Bake on the middle shelf of the oven for 20 minutes.

MEANWHILE, mix the chopped fennel fronds with the capers and shallot. Season the inside of the trout and fill with the fennel and caper stuffing. Put the bay leaf, cubes of butter and the lemon slices inside the fish too. Mix together the fish stock and vermouth.

REMOVE the vegetables from the oven, stir well and reduce the oven temperature to 140°C (275°F/Gas 1). Lay the trout over the vegetables and pour the stock and vermouth over the fish. Season the trout and drizzle with the remaining tablespoon of olive oil. Cover the top of the tin with foil and return to the oven for 1^1/$_4$ hours or until the fish is cooked through. The flesh should feel flaky through the skin and the inside will look opaque and cooked. Lift the fish onto a large serving platter.

TRANSFER the roasting tin of vegetables to the stove top and heat for a couple of minutes, until the juices bubble and reduce. Now add the cream and cook for 1 minute, then stir in the chervil and season to taste. Spoon the vegetables around the fish on the platter, pour over a little of the juice and hand around the rest separately in a jug.

Stuffing the trout allows the flavours to permeate the flesh. Use the vegetables as a rack for the fish to lie on.

Marseille fish market buildings.

MARMITE DIEPPOISE

THIS RICH SOUPY STEW OF SHELLFISH AND FISH GIVES AWAY ITS ORIGINS IN THE NORMANDY REGION BY ITS USE OF CIDER AND CREAM. TRADITIONALLY TURBOT AND SOLE ARE USED, BUT THE SALMON ADDS A SPLASH OF COLOUR.

16 mussels
12 large prawns (shrimp)
500 ml (2 cups) cider or dry white
  wine
50 g (1³/₄ oz) butter
1 garlic clove, crushed
2 French shallots, finely chopped
2 celery stalks, finely chopped
1 large leek, white part only, thinly
  sliced
250 g (9 oz) small chestnut
  mushrooms, sliced
1 bay leaf
300 g (10¹/₂ oz) salmon fillet,
  skinned and cut into chunks
400 g (14 oz) sole fillet, skinned and
  cut into thick strips widthways
315 ml (1¹/₄ cups) thick
  (double/heavy) cream
3 tablespoons finely chopped
  parsley

SERVES 6

SCRUB the mussels and remove their beards. Throw away any that are already open and don't close when tapped on the work surface. Peel and devein the prawns.

POUR the cider or white wine into a large saucepan and bring to a simmer. Add the mussels, cover the pan and cook for 3–5 minutes, shaking the pan every now and then. Place a fine sieve over a bowl and tip the mussels into the sieve. Transfer the mussels to a plate, throwing away any that haven't opened in the cooking time. Strain the cooking liquid again through the sieve, leaving behind any grit or sand.

ADD the butter to the cleaned saucepan and melt over moderate heat. Add the garlic, shallot, celery and leek and cook for 7–10 minutes, or until the vegetables are just soft. Add the mushrooms and cook for a further 4–5 minutes, until softened. While the vegetables are cooking, remove the mussels from their shells.

ADD the strained liquid to the vegetables in the saucepan, add the bay leaf and bring to a simmer. Add the salmon, sole and prawns and cook for 3–4 minutes until the fish is opaque and the prawns have turned pink. Stir in the cream and cooked mussels and simmer gently for 2 minutes. Season to taste and stir in the parsley.

Tip the cooked mussels into a sieve and throw away any that haven't opened. Make a sauce of the vegetables and poaching liquid, then add the seafood to cook quickly at the end.

Salt cod on sale in a Paris market.

Add the cream and oil alternately, beating until the brandade has the consistency of fluffy mash.

BRANDADE DE MORUE

THIS RICH GARLICKY PURÉE IS TRADITIONALLY MADE WITH *MORUE*, SALT COD PRESERVED BY THE SALT RATHER THAN BY DRYING. SALT COD IS ALSO SOLD AS BACALAO, ITS SPANISH NAME. YOU WILL HAVE TO PREPARE TWO DAYS IN ADVANCE, BECAUSE OF THE TIME NEEDED TO SOAK THE COD.

750 g (1 lb 10 oz) piece salt cod
(also known as *morue*)
315 ml (1¼ cups) olive oil
2 garlic cloves, crushed
315 ml (1¼ cups) cream
2 tablespoons lemon juice

SERVES 4

PUT the salt cod in a shallow bowl and cover with cold water. Refrigerate for 1 or 2 days, changing the water every 8 hours, to soak the salt out of the fish.

DRAIN the cod and rinse again. Put in a saucepan and cover with 2 litres (8 cups) water. Bring to a simmer and cook for 10 minutes (do not boil or the salt cod will toughen). Drain and rinse again.

REMOVE the skin and bones from the cod. Use a fork to flake the cod into small pieces. Make sure there are no small bones left in the cod, then finely chop in a food processor or with a sharp knife. (It will have a fibrous texture.)

HEAT 60 ml (¼ cup) of the oil in a heavy-based frying pan and cook the garlic over low heat for 3 minutes without colouring. Add the cod and stir in a spoonful of the remaining oil. Beat in a spoonful of cream and continue adding the oil and cream alternately, beating until the mixture is smooth and has the consistency of fluffy mashed potato. Add the lemon juice and season with pepper (you won't need to add any salt). Serve warm or cold with bread or toast. Keep in the fridge for up to 3 days and warm through with a little extra cream before serving.

PIKE QUENELLES

PIKE QUENELLES ARE A SPECIALITY OF THE LYON REGION. QUENELLES ARE SMALL OVAL BALLS OF CHOPPED FISH OR MEAT, USUALLY COOKED BY POACHING. THEY CAN BE A LITTLE TRICKY TO MAKE— THE KEY LIES IN KEEPING THE MIXTURE CHILLED. IF PIKE IS UNAVAILABLE, SOLE DOES WELL.

450 g (1 lb) pike fillet, bones and skin removed
2 tablespoons finely chopped parsley
200 ml (7 fl oz) milk
80 g (2/3 cup) plain (all-purpose) flour
2 large eggs, lightly beaten
150 g (5¹/2 oz) butter, softened and cubed
2 large egg whites
200 ml (7 fl oz) thick (double/heavy) cream
1 litre (4 cups) fish stock

SAUCE
50 g (1³/4 oz) butter
40 g (1/3 cup) plain (all-purpose) flour
400 ml (14 fl oz) milk
80 ml (1/3 cup) thick (double/heavy) cream
large pinch of grated nutmeg
65 g (1/2 cup) grated Gruyère cheese

SERVES 6

POUND the fish to a paste in a pestle and mortar, or purée in a food processor. Transfer to a mixing bowl, stir in the parsley, cover and refrigerate.

PUT the milk in a saucepan and bring just to boiling point. Take the saucepan off the heat and add all the flour. Return to gentle heat and beat in the flour, then take the pan off the heat and leave to cool. Using electric beaters or a wooden spoon, gradually add the eggs, beating after each addition. Add the butter, piece by piece, then stir the mixture into the fish purée, cover and chill.

WHEN the mixture is very cold, put the bowl inside a larger bowl filled with ice cubes. Gradually and alternately, add the egg whites and cream, beating after each addition. Season generously, cover and chill again.

TO MAKE the sauce, melt the butter in a saucepan, then stir in the flour to make a roux. Cook, stirring constantly, for 2 minutes without allowing the roux to brown. Remove from the heat and gradually add the milk, stirring after each addition until smooth. Return to the heat and bring to the boil. Simmer for 2 minutes, add the cream and season with nutmeg, salt and pepper.

USING TWO tablespoons, mould the fish mixture into 30 egg shapes (quenelles) and put on a buttered baking tray in the fridge for 20 minutes. Heat the fish stock in a large frying pan until barely simmering and gently lower the quenelles into the liquid in batches. Poach for 5–7 minutes, or until the quenelles rise to the surface and feel firm to the touch. At no stage should the poaching liquid boil. Use a slotted spoon to gently lift the quenelles into six lightly buttered gratin dishes. Preheat the grill (broiler). Pour the sauce over the quenelles and scatter with the cheese. Grill until brown and bubbling.

Dairy herd in the Alpine foothills.

Pound the fish to a paste and then stir in the parsley.

SALMON EN PAPILLOTE WITH HERB SAUCE

4 x 200 g (7 oz) salmon fillets,
skinned
10 g (¹/₄ oz) butter, melted
8 thin slices of lemon, halved

HERB SAUCE
315 ml (1¹/₄ cups) fish stock
80 ml (¹/₃ cup) dry white wine
2 French shallots, finely chopped
250 ml (1 cup) thick (double/heavy)
cream
4 tablespoons finely chopped herbs
such as chervil, chives, parsley,
tarragon or sorrel

SERVES 4

PREHEAT the oven to 200°C (400°F/Gas 6).

REMOVE ANY bones from the salmon fillets: you
may need to use tweezers to do this. Cut out four
30 cm (12 inch) greaseproof paper circles. Fold
each circle in half, then open out again and brush
with melted butter. Place a salmon fillet on one half
of each paper circle, lay four half slices of lemon
on top, season, then fold the other half of the
paper over the fish to enclose it. Seal the parcels
by folding the two edges of greaseproof paper
tightly together. Put on a baking tray and bake for
10–15 minutes (depending on the thickness of the
salmon), or until the fish is firm to the touch.

TO MAKE the herb sauce, put the stock, wine
and shallots in a pan and simmer until the mixture
has reduced to a syrup (you should have about
5 tablespoons of liquid left). Add the cream and
bubble for a few minutes to thicken slightly.
Season and gently stir in the herbs. Serve each
diner a parcel to unwrap at the table with the herb
sauce in a separate bowl.

Wrap the pieces of salmon in
large circles of greaseproof
paper to seal in the flavours while
they bake.

SKATE WITH BLACK BUTTER

COURT BOUILLON
250 ml (1 cup) white wine
1 onion, sliced
1 carrot, sliced
1 bay leaf
4 black peppercorns

4 x 250 g (9 oz) skate wings,
skinned
100 g (3¹/₂ oz) unsalted butter
1 tablespoon chopped parsley
1 tablespoon capers, rinsed,
squeezed dry and chopped

SERVES 4

TO MAKE the court bouillon, put the wine, onion,
carrot, bay leaf, peppercorns and 1 litre (4 cups)
water into a large deep frying pan, bring to the
boil and simmer for 20 minutes. Strain the court
bouillon and return to the cleaned frying pan.

ADD the skate and simmer for 10 minutes, or until
it flakes when tested with the point of a knife. Lift
out the fish, drain, cover and keep warm.

HEAT the butter in a frying pan and cook over
moderate heat for 2 minutes until it turns brown
to make a *beurre noisette*. Remove from the heat
and stir in the parsley, capers, salt and pepper.

POUR the sauce over the top of the fish and
serve immediately. You can lift the fillet off each
side of the fish first, if you prefer.

SKATE WITH BLACK BUTTER

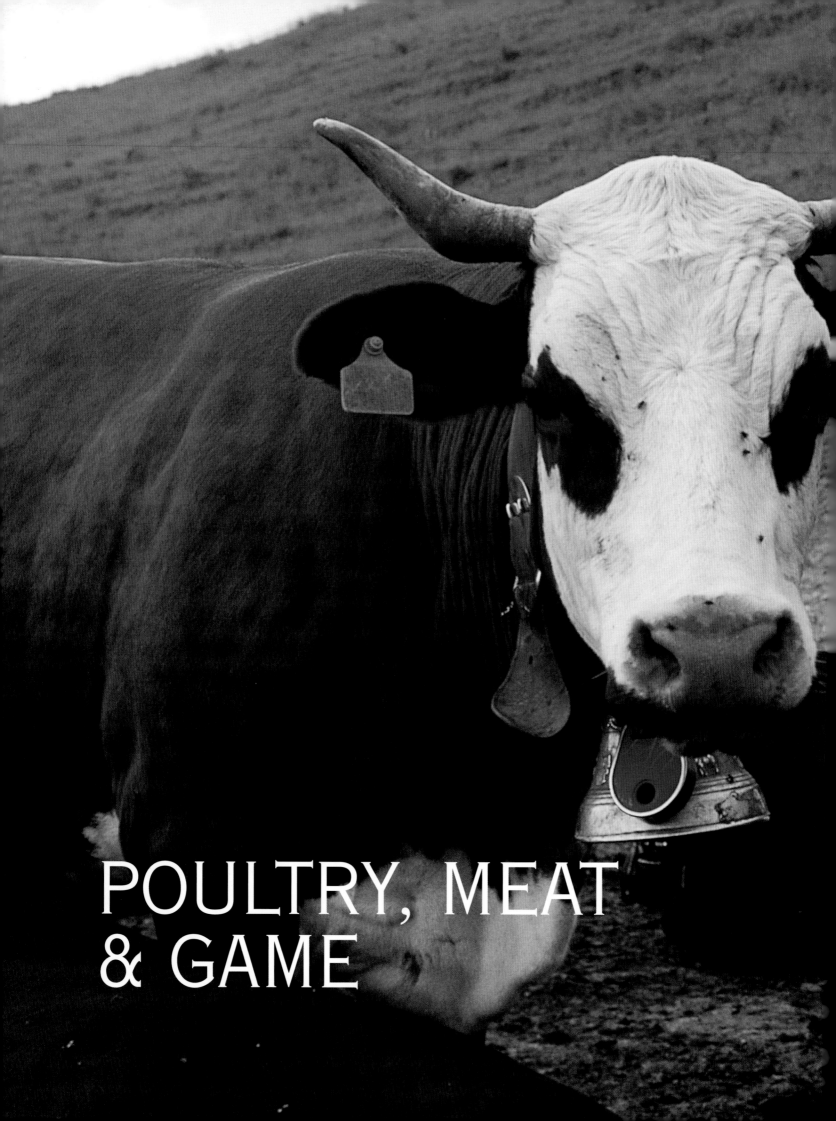

POULTRY, MEAT & GAME

COQ AU VIN

A DISH ALLEGEDLY PREPARED BY CAESAR WHEN BATTLING THE GAULS, WHO SENT HIM A SCRAWNY CHICKEN AS A MESSAGE OF DEFIANCE. CAESAR COOKED IT IN WINE AND HERBS AND INVITED THEM TO EAT, THUS DEMONSTRATING THE OVERWHELMING SOPHISTICATION OF THE ROMANS.

2 x 1.6 kg (3 lb 8 oz) chickens
1 bottle red wine
2 bay leaves
2 sprigs of thyme
250 g (9 oz) bacon, diced
60 g (2¼ oz) butter
20 pickling or pearl onions
250 g (9 oz) button mushrooms
1 teaspoon oil
30 g (¼ cup) plain (all-purpose) flour
1 litre (4 cups) chicken stock
125 ml (½ cup) brandy
2 teaspoons tomato paste (purée)
1½ tablespoons softened butter
1 tablespoon plain (all-purpose) flour
2 tablespoons chopped parsley

SERVES 8

JOINT EACH chicken into eight pieces by removing both legs and cutting between the joint of the drumstick and the thigh. Cut down either side of the backbone and lift it out. Turn the chicken over and cut through the cartilage down the centre of the breastbone. Cut each breast in half, leaving the wing attached to the top half.

PUT the wine, bay leaves, thyme and some salt and pepper in a bowl and add the chicken. Cover and leave to marinate, preferably overnight.

BLANCH the bacon in boiling water, then drain, pat dry and sauté in a frying pan until golden. Lift out onto a plate. Melt a quarter of the butter in the pan, add the onions and sauté until browned. Lift out and set aside.

MELT another quarter of the butter, add the mushrooms, season with salt and pepper and sauté for 5 minutes. Remove and set aside.

DRAIN the chicken, reserving the marinade, and pat the chicken dry. Season. Add the remaining butter and the oil to the frying pan, add the chicken and sauté until golden. Stir in the flour.

TRANSFER the chicken to a large saucepan or casserole and add the stock. Pour the brandy into the frying pan and boil, stirring, for 30 seconds to deglaze the pan. Pour over the chicken. Add the marinade, onions, mushrooms, bacon and tomato paste. Cook over moderate heat for 45 minutes, or until the chicken is cooked through.

IF the sauce needs thickening, lift out the chicken and vegetables and bring the sauce to the boil. Mix together the butter and flour to make a *beurre manié* and whisk into the sauce. Boil, stirring, for 2 minutes until thickened. Add the parsley and return the chicken and vegetables to the sauce.

Cooking the chicken with the skin on keeps the flesh moist.

CHICKEN WITH FORTY CLOVES OF GARLIC

THIS SOUNDS FRIGHTENINGLY OVERPOWERING BUT, AS ANYONE WHO HAS EVER ROASTED GARLIC

KNOWS, THE CLOVES MELLOW AND SWEETEN IN THE OVEN UNTIL, WHEN YOU COME TO SERVE, THE

CREAMY FLESH THAT IS SQUEEZED FROM THE SKINS IS QUITE DIFFERENT FROM THE RAW CLOVE.

2 celery stalks, including leaves
2 sprigs of rosemary
4 sprigs of thyme
4 sprigs of flat-leaf (Italian) parsley
1 x 1.6 kg (3 lb 8 oz) chicken
40 garlic cloves, unpeeled
2 tablespoons olive oil
1 carrot, roughly chopped
1 small onion, cut into 4 wedges
250 ml (1 cup) white wine
1 baguette, cut into slices
small sprigs of herbs, to garnish

SERVES 4

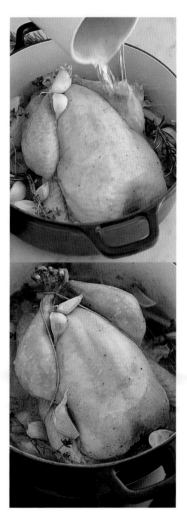

PREHEAT the oven to 200°C (400°F/Gas 6). Put a chopped celery stalk and 2 sprigs each of the rosemary, thyme and parsley into the chicken cavity. Add 6 cloves of garlic. Tie the legs together and tuck the wing tips under.

BRUSH the chicken liberally with some of the oil and season well. Scatter about 10 more garlic cloves over the base of a large casserole dish. Put the remaining sprigs of herbs, chopped celery, carrot and onion in the casserole.

PUT the chicken in the dish. Scatter the remaining garlic cloves around the chicken and add the remaining oil and the wine. Cover and bake for 1 hour 20 minutes, or until the chicken is tender and the juices run clear when the thigh is pierced with a skewer.

TO SERVE, carefully lift the chicken out of the casserole dish. Strain off the juices into a small saucepan. Use tongs to pick out the garlic cloves from the strained mixture. Spoon off the fat from the juices and boil for 2–3 minutes to reduce and thicken a little.

CUT the chicken into serving portions, pour over a little of the juices and scatter with the garlic. Toast the baguette slices, then garnish the chicken with herb sprigs and serve with the bread to be spread with the soft flesh squeezed from the garlic.

Use a casserole dish into which the chicken and vegetables fit quite snugly so that the flavours mingle well.

CHICKEN CHASSEUR

CHASSEUR MEANS 'HUNTER' AND IS USED FOR DISHES INCLUDING MUSHROOMS, SHALLOTS, TOMATOES, WINE AND BRANDY. THE NAME PROBABLY REFERS TO THE FACT THAT THIS WAS ORIGINALLY A RECIPE FOR COOKING GAME.

1 x 1.6 kg (3 lb 8 oz) chicken
1 tablespoon oil
60 g (2¹/₄ oz) butter
2 French shallots, finely chopped
125 g (4¹/₂ oz) button mushrooms, sliced
1 tablespoon plain (all-purpose) flour
125 ml (¹/₂ cup) white wine
2 tablespoons brandy
2 teaspoons tomato paste (purée)
250 ml (1 cup) chicken stock
2 teaspoons chopped tarragon
1 teaspoon chopped parsley

CROUTONS
2 slices bread
olive oil

SERVES 4

JOINT the chicken into eight pieces by removing both legs and cutting between the joint of the drumstick and the thigh. Cut down either side of the backbone and lift it out. Turn the chicken over and cut through the cartilage down the centre of the breastbone. Cut each breast in half, leaving the wing attached to the top half.

HEAT the oil in a frying pan or saucepan and add half the butter. When the foaming subsides, add the chicken and sauté in batches on both sides until browned. Lift out onto a plate and keep warm. Pour the excess fat out of the pan.

MELT the remaining butter in the pan, add the shallots and cook gently until softened but not browned. Add the mushrooms and cook, covered, over moderate heat for 3 minutes.

ADD the flour and cook, stirring constantly, for 1 minute. Stir in the white wine, brandy, tomato paste and stock. Bring to the boil, stirring constantly, then reduce the heat and add the tarragon. Season.

RETURN the chicken to the pan, cover and simmer for 30 minutes, or until the chicken is tender and cooked through. Sprinkle with parsley to serve.

TO MAKE the croutons, trim the crusts from the bread and cut the bread into moon shapes with a biscuit cutter. Heat the olive oil in a frying pan and fry the bread until golden. Drain the croutons on paper towels and serve hot with the chicken.

TARRAGON CHICKEN

TARRAGON HAS A DELICATE, BUT DISTINCTIVE, LIQUORICE FLAVOUR AND IS ONE OF THE HERBS THAT GOES INTO THE FRENCH *FINES HERBES* MIXTURE. IT IS KNOWN AS A PARTICULARLY GOOD PARTNER FOR CHICKEN, WITH A TARRAGON CREAM SAUCE MAKING A CLASSIC COMBINATION.

1¹/₂ tablespoons chopped tarragon
1 small garlic clove, crushed
50 g (1³/₄ oz) butter, softened
1 x 1.6 kg (3 lb 8 oz) chicken
2 teaspoons oil
170 ml (²/₃ cup) chicken stock
2 tablespoons white wine
1 tablespoon plain (all-purpose) flour
1 tablespoon tarragon leaves
170 ml (²/₃ cup) thick
    (double/heavy) cream

SERVES 4

PREHEAT the oven to 200°C (400°F/Gas 6). Mix together the chopped tarragon, garlic and half the butter. Season with salt and pepper and place inside the cavity of the chicken. Tie the legs together and tuck the wing tips under.

HEAT the remaining butter with the oil in a large casserole dish over low heat and brown the chicken on all sides. Add the chicken stock and wine. Cover the casserole and bake in the oven for 1 hour 20 minutes, or until the chicken is tender and the juices run clear when the thigh is pierced with a skewer. Remove the chicken, draining all the juices back into the casserole. Cover with foil and a tea towel and leave the chicken to rest.

SKIM a tablespoon of the surface fat from the cooking liquid and put it in a small bowl. Skim the remainder of the fat from the surface and throw this away. Add the flour to the reserved fat and mix until smooth. Whisk quickly into the cooking liquid and stir over moderate heat until the sauce boils and thickens.

STRAIN the sauce into a clean saucepan and add the tarragon leaves. Simmer for 2 minutes, then stir in the cream and reheat without boiling. Season with salt and pepper. Carve the chicken and spoon the sauce over the top to serve.

Brown the chicken to seal before adding the stock and wine.

Buying cooked chickens and meat from a market rotisserie.

TARRAGON CHICKEN

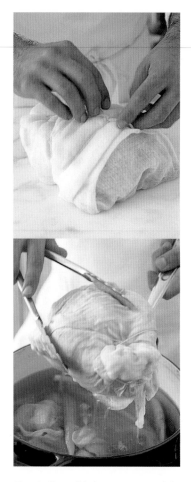

POULE AU POT

WHEN HENRY IV WISHED THAT ALL HIS SUBJECTS HAVE A CHICKEN FOR THEIR POT EVERY SUNDAY, THIS WAS PRESUMABLY THE MEAL HE HAD IN MIND. THE CHICKEN IS COOKED SIMPLY, SO IT IS IMPERATIVE TO USE A FREE-RANGE BIRD FOR THE BEST FLAVOUR.

1 x 1.6 kg (3 lb 8 oz) chicken
1 carrot, roughly chopped
1/2 onion, halved
1 celery stalk, roughly chopped
1 garlic clove
4 sprigs of parsley
2 bay leaves
8 black peppercorns
8 juniper berries
2 bacon bones
1 teaspoon salt
12 baby carrots
8 baby leeks
8 baby turnips
12 small new potatoes

SERVES 4

SEASON the chicken and wrap it up in muslin, securing with string. Put into a large saucepan. Tie the carrot, onion, celery, garlic, parsley, bay leaves, peppercorns and juniper berries in another piece of muslin and add to the saucepan. Add the bacon bones and salt, cover with cold water and bring to simmering point. Cook over very low heat for 40 minutes.

TRIM the baby vegetables, add to the saucepan and cook for 10 more minutes. Lift out the chicken and drain on a wire rack over a tray. Cook the vegetables for a further 10 minutes. Remove the skin from the chicken and carve, then serve with the cooked vegetables. Strain the cooking liquid, discarding the bacon bones, and serve as a broth to start the meal or freeze for soup stock.

Cook the chicken wrapped in muslin to help it keep its shape.

POULET RÔTI

50 g (1³/4 oz) butter, softened
1 x 1.6 kg (3 lb 8 oz) chicken
1 sprig of tarragon or rosemary
310 ml (1¹/4 cups) chicken stock

SERVES 4

PREHEAT the oven to 200°C (400°F/Gas 6). Place half the butter inside the chicken with the tarragon or rosemary. Rub the chicken with the remaining butter and season. Tie the legs together and tuck the wing tips under. Put, breast side down, in a roasting tin and add the stock.

COVER the chicken loosely with foil and roast for 30 minutes, basting occasionally. Uncover, turn the chicken and roast for 30–40 minutes, or until golden brown and the juices run clear when the thigh is pierced with a skewer.

REMOVE the chicken from the tin, cover with foil and a tea towel and leave to rest. Put the tin on the stove top and skim off most of the fat. Boil rapidly until the juices reduce and become syrupy. Strain and serve with the chicken.

POULET RÔTI

POULET VALLÉE D'AUGE

THIS IS ONE OF THE CLASSIC DISHES OF NORMANDY AND BRITTANY, THE APPLE-GROWING REGIONS OF FRANCE. IF YOU HEAR IT REFERRED TO AS *POULET AU CIDRE*, THIS MEANS THE CHICKEN HAS BEEN COOKED IN CIDER RATHER THAN STOCK.

1 x 1.6 kg (3 lb 8 oz) chicken
2 dessert apples
1 tablespoon lemon juice
60 g (2¼ oz) butter
½ onion, finely chopped
½ celery stalk, finely chopped
1 tablespoon plain (all-purpose) flour
80 ml (⅓ cup) Calvados or brandy
375 ml (1½ cups) chicken stock
80 ml (⅓ cup) crème fraîche

SERVES 4

JOINT the chicken into eight pieces by removing both legs and cutting between the joint of the drumstick and the thigh. Cut down either side of the backbone and lift it out. Turn the chicken over and cut through the cartilage down the centre of the breastbone. Cut each breast in half, leaving the wing attached to the top half.

PEEL and core the apples. Finely chop half of one apple and cut the rest into 12 wedges. Toss the apple in the lemon juice.

HEAT half the butter in a large frying pan, then add the chicken pieces, skin side down, and cook until golden. Turn over and cook for another 5 minutes. Lift the chicken out of the pan and tip away the fat.

HEAT 1 tablespoon more butter in the same pan, add the onion, celery and chopped apple and fry over moderate heat for 5 minutes without browning.

REMOVE from the heat. Sprinkle the flour over the vegetables and stir in. Add the Calvados and return to the heat. Gradually stir in the chicken stock. Bring to the boil, return the chicken to the pan, cover and simmer gently for 15 minutes, or until the chicken is tender and cooked through.

MEANWHILE, heat the remaining butter in a small frying pan. Add the apple wedges and fry over moderate heat until browned and tender. Remove from the pan and keep warm.

Fry the chopped apple with the chicken and its sauce, to give flavour and then fry the apple wedges separately.

REMOVE the chicken from the pan and keep warm. Skim the excess fat from the cooking liquid. Add the crème fraîche, bring to the boil and boil for 4 minutes, or until the sauce is thick enough to lightly coat the back of a wooden spoon. Season and pour over the chicken. Serve with the apple wedges.

DUCK BREASTS WITH CASSIS AND RASPBERRIES

MAGRET IS THE FRENCH NAME FOR DUCK BREAST, THE LEANEST PORTION OF THE DUCK. *MAGRET DE CANARD* IS USUALLY SERVED PINK WITH A WELL-CRISPED SKIN. YOU CAN USE FROZEN RASPBERRIES FOR THIS RECIPE, BUT MAKE SURE THEY ARE THOROUGHLY DEFROSTED.

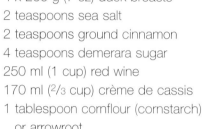

4 x 200 g (7 oz) duck breasts
2 teaspoons sea salt
2 teaspoons ground cinnamon
4 teaspoons demerara sugar
250 ml (1 cup) red wine
170 ml (²/₃ cup) crème de cassis
1 tablespoon cornflour (cornstarch)
   or arrowroot
250 g (9 oz) raspberries

SERVES 4

SCORE the duck breasts through the skin and fat but not all the way through to the meat. Heat a frying pan and fry the duck breasts, skin side down, until the skin browns and the fat runs out. Lift the breasts out of the pan and tip away most of the fat.

MIX TOGETHER the sea salt, cinnamon and demerara sugar. Sprinkle over the skin of the duck breasts, then press in with your hands. Season with black pepper. Reheat the frying pan and cook the duck breasts, skin side up, for 10–15 minutes. Lift out of the frying pan and leave to rest on a carving board. Preheat the grill (broiler).

MEANWHILE, mix together the red wine and cassis in a jug. Pour about 80 ml (¹/₃ cup) of the liquid into a small bowl and mix in the cornflour or arrowroot, then pour this back into the jug.

POUR the excess fat out of the frying pan to leave about 2 tablespoons. Return the pan to the heat and pour in the red wine and cassis. Simmer for 2–3 minutes, stirring constantly, until the sauce has thickened. Add the raspberries and simmer for another minute, to warm the fruit through. Check the seasoning.

GRILL the duck breasts, skin side up, for a minute, or until the sugar starts to caramelize. Slice the duck breasts thinly, pour a little sauce over the top and serve the rest separately in a jug.

DUCK A L'ORANGE

DUCK CAN BE FATTY, WHICH IS WHY IT SHOULD BE PRICKED ALL OVER AND COOKED ON A RACK TO LET THE FAT DRAIN AWAY. THE REASON THAT DUCK A L'ORANGE WORKS SO PERFECTLY AS A DISH, IS THAT THE SWEET ACIDITY OF THE CITRUS FRUIT CUTS THROUGH THE RICH DUCK FAT.

5 oranges
1 x 2 kg (4 lb 8 oz) duck
2 cinnamon sticks
15 g (1/2 oz) mint leaves
95 g (1/2 cup) light brown sugar
125 ml (1/2 cup) cider vinegar
80 ml (1/3 cup) Grand Marnier
30 g (1 oz) butter

SERVES 4

PREHEAT the oven to 150°C (300°F/Gas 2). Halve two of the oranges and rub them all over the duck. Place them inside the duck cavity with the cinnamon sticks and mint. Tie the legs together and tie the wings together. Prick all over with a fork so that the fat can drain out as the duck cooks.

PUT the duck on a rack, breast side down, and put the rack in a shallow roasting tin. Roast for 45 minutes, turning the duck halfway through.

MEANWHILE, zest and juice the remaining oranges (if you don't have a zester, cut the orange peel into thin strips with a sharp knife). Heat the sugar in a saucepan over low heat until it melts and then caramelizes: swirl the pan gently to make sure it caramelizes evenly. When the sugar is a rich brown, add the vinegar (be careful as it will splutter) and boil for 3 minutes. Add the orange juice and Grand Marnier and simmer for 2 minutes.

Adding the orange juice to the caramel sauce.

BLANCH the orange zest in boiling water for 1 minute, three times, changing the water each time. Refresh under cold water, drain and reserve.

REMOVE the excess fat from the tin. Increase the oven temperature to 180°C (350°F/Gas 4). Spoon some of the orange sauce over the duck and roast for 45 minutes, spooning the remaining sauce over the duck every 5 to 10 minutes and turning the duck to baste all sides.

REMOVE the duck from the oven, cover with foil and strain the juices back into a saucepan. Skim off any excess fat and add the orange zest and butter to the saucepan. Stir to melt the butter. Reheat the sauce and serve over the duck.

A butcher's shop in Paris.

DUCKLING WITH TURNIPS

1 x 1.8 kg (4 lb) duckling
bouquet garni
30 g (1 oz) clarified butter
1 carrot, chopped
1 celery stalk, chopped
1/2 large onion, chopped
2 teaspoons sugar
8 French shallots
8 baby turnips
80 ml (1/3 cup) white wine
500 ml (2 cups) chicken stock
2 teaspoons softened butter
2 teaspoons plain (all-purpose) flour

SERVES 2

The white wine and stock in the roasting tin adds flavour and helps to keep the duckling moist.

PREHEAT the oven to 200°C (400°F/Gas 6) and put a roasting tin in the oven to heat up. Truss the duckling by tying the legs together and tying the wing tips together behind the body. Prick all over, put the bouquet garni in the cavity and season.

HEAT the clarified butter in a large frying pan and brown the duckling on both sides. Lift the duckling out of the pan and pour all but a tablespoon of the fat into a jug. Add the carrot, celery and onion to the pan and soften over the heat, then brown. Remove the vegetables.

ADD ANOTHER 2 tablespoons of duck fat to the pan. Add the sugar and let it dissolve over low heat. Turn up the heat and add the shallots and turnips. Caramelize over high heat, then remove from the pan. Pour in the white wine and boil, stirring, for 30 seconds to deglaze the pan.

PUT the carrot, celery and onion in the middle of the hot roasting tin, place the duckling on top and pour in the white wine and stock. Add the turnips to the tin and roast for 45 minutes. Baste well, add the shallots and roast for another 20 minutes. Baste again and roast for a further 25 minutes.

LIFT OUT the duck, turnips and shallots and keep warm. Strain the sauce, pressing the chopped vegetables in the sieve to extract all the juices, then throw away the chopped vegetables.

POUR the strained sauce into a saucepan and boil rapidly to reduce by half. Mix together the butter and flour to make a *beurre manié*. Whisk into the sauce and boil, stirring, for 2 minutes until thickened.

PUT the duckling, turnips and shallots on a serving plate and pour a little sauce over them. Serve the rest of the sauce in a jug.

DUCK CONFIT

A CONFIT IS THE TRADITIONAL METHOD OF PRESERVING MEAT FOR USE THROUGHOUT THE YEAR. TODAY IT IS STILL A DELICIOUS WAY TO COOK AND EAT DUCK. THE THIGHS AND LEGS ARE USUALLY PRESERVED, WITH THE BREAST BEING SERVED FRESH.

8 large duck legs
8 tablespoons coarse sea salt
12 bay leaves
8 sprigs of thyme
16 juniper berries, lightly crushed
2 kg (4 lb 8 oz) duck or goose fat,
　　cut into pieces

SERVES 8

PUT the duck legs in a bowl or dish in which they fit snuggly. Scatter the salt over the top, season with black pepper and tuck half the bay leaves, thyme sprigs and juniper berries into the dish. Cover and leave in the fridge overnight.

PREHEAT the oven to 180°C (350°F/Gas 4). Put the duck legs in a large roasting tin, leaving behind the herbs and any liquid that has formed in the bottom of the bowl. Add the duck or goose fat to the tin and roast for 1 hour. Reduce the oven to 150°C (300°F/Gas 2) and roast the duck for a further 2 hours, basting occasionally, until the duck is very well cooked.

WASH one large (or two smaller) kilner jars and dry in the hot oven for 5 minutes to sterilize them. Use tongs to put the hot duck legs into the hot jar and add the remaining bay leaves, thyme sprigs and juniper berries. Strain the cooking fat through a sieve and into a large jug. Now pour the fat into the jar to cover the duck. Close the lid and leave to cool. The fat will solidify on cooling.

Use tongs to push the duck legs into the jars, then cover with the strained hot fat to seal.

DUCK CONFIT will keep for several months in a cool pantry or fridge. To use, remove as much duck as you need from the jar, returning any excess fat to cover the remaining duck. The meat can then be roasted in a very hot oven until really crisp and served with lentils, beans or salad. Or the duck can be used to make cassoulet.

Confit de canard is used to add richness to cassoulet.

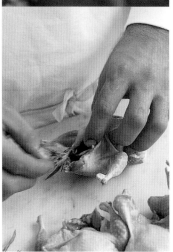

QUAILS WITH GRAPES AND TARRAGON

8 sprigs of tarragon
8 x 150 g (5¹/₂ oz) quails
2 tablespoons clarified butter
170 ml (²/₃ cup) white wine
410 ml (1²/₃ cups) chicken stock
150 g (5¹/₂ oz) seedless green
  grapes

SERVES 4

PUT a sprig of tarragon into the cavity of each quail and season well. Heat the clarified butter in a sauté pan or deep frying pan and brown the quails on all sides. Add the wine and boil for 30 seconds, then add the stock and grapes.

COVER the pan and simmer for 8 minutes or until the quails are cooked through. Lift out the quails and grapes and keep warm. Boil the sauce until it has reduced by two-thirds and become syrupy. Strain the sauce and pour over the quails and grapes to serve.

Push a fresh tarragon sprig into each quail before cooking, so that the flavour infuses the flesh.

PRUNE AND WALNUT-STUFFED SPATCHCOCKS

FRENCH AGEN PRUNES ARE SAID TO BE THE BEST IN THE WORLD AND THE COMBINATION OF PRUNES WITH WALNUTS IS A CLASSIC ONE, WITH BOTH THE FRUIT AND THE NUTS COMING FROM THE SAME AREA OF SOUTHWEST FRANCE.

STUFFING
10 g (¹/₄ oz) butter
4 French shallots, finely chopped
1 large garlic clove, crushed
70 g (2¹/₂ oz) shelled walnuts,
  chopped
14 prunes, pitted and chopped

4 spatchcocks (poussins)
4 bay leaves
4 rashers streaky bacon
50 g (1³/₄ oz) butter
juice of 1 small lemon
2 tablespoons honey
60 ml (¹/₄ cup) thick (double/heavy)
  cream or crème fraîche

SERVES 4

TO MAKE the stuffing, heat the butter in a frying pan, add the shallot and cook for 10–15 minutes. Add the garlic and cook for 1 minute. Remove the pan from the heat and stir in the walnuts and prunes. Season and leave to cool. Preheat the oven to 180°C (350°F/Gas 4).

SPOON an equal amount of stuffing into each spatchcock, then add a bay leaf. Tie the legs together and tuck the wing tips under. Arrange the spatchcock in a roasting tin and wrap a rasher of bacon around each spatchcock breast.

PLACE the butter in a small pan with the lemon juice and honey. Melt together, then pour over the spatchcocks. Roast, basting often, for 45 minutes, or until a skewer pushed into the centre of the stuffing comes out too hot to touch.

LIFT the spatchcocks out of the tin, cover and keep warm. Put the roasting tin on the stove top, heat until the juices bubble and stir in the cream or crème fraîche. Season the sauce, pour a little over the spatchcocks and serve the rest separately.

PRUNE AND WALNUT-STUFFED
SPATCHCOCKS

148

VENISON WITH BLACKBERRY SAUCE

60 g (2¼ oz) clarified butter
12 pickling or pearl onions
150 g (5½ oz) blackberries or
 blackcurrants
3 tablespoons redcurrant jelly
16 x 50 g (1¾ oz) venison
 medallions
60 ml (¼ cup) red wine
410 ml (1⅔ cups) brown stock
2 teaspoons softened butter
2 teaspoons plain (all-purpose) flour

SERVES 4

HEAT half the clarified butter in a saucepan. Add the onions, cover with crumpled wet greaseproof paper and a lid. Cook gently for 20–25 minutes, stirring occasionally, until brown and cooked. Put the berries in a saucepan with the redcurrant jelly and 3 tablespoons water. Boil for 5 minutes until the fruit is softened and the liquid syrupy.

SEASON the venison, heat the remaining clarified butter in a frying pan and cook in batches over high heat for 1–2 minutes. Remove the venison and keep warm. Add the wine to the pan and boil for 30 seconds. Add the stock and boil until reduced by half.

MIX TOGETHER the butter and flour to make a *beurre manié* and whisk into the stock. Boil, stirring, for 2 minutes, then drain the syrup from the fruit into the stock to make a sauce. Stir well, season and serve with the venison and onions. Use the drained fruit as a garnish if you like.

Brown the venison in batches so that it fries without stewing. Drain the syrup from the fruit to add flavour to the sauce.

ROASTED PHEASANT WITH GARLIC AND SHALLOTS

1 x 1 kg (2 lb 4 oz) pheasant
½ teaspoon juniper or allspice
 berries, lightly crushed
a few sprigs of parsley
30 g (1 oz) butter
6 rashers streaky bacon
6 French shallots, unpeeled
6 garlic cloves, unpeeled
1 teaspoon plain (all-purpose) flour
80 ml (⅓ cup) chicken stock

SERVES 2

PREHEAT the oven to 200°C (400°F/Gas 6). Rub the pheasant with salt, pepper and the juniper berries. Fill the cavity with the parsley and butter, tie the legs together and tuck the wing tips under. Place in a small roasting tin and lay the bacon over the pheasant to prevent it drying out. Scatter with the unpeeled shallots and garlic and roast for 20 minutes. Remove the bacon and roast for a further 10 minutes.

REMOVE the shallots, garlic and pheasant from the tin and cut off the pheasant legs. Put the legs back in the tin and cook for another 5 minutes, then remove and keep all the pheasant warm.

TO MAKE the gravy, transfer the roasting tin to the stovetop. Stir in the flour and cook, stirring, for 2 minutes. Add the stock and bring to the boil, whisking constantly. Boil for 2 minutes to thicken slightly, then strain the gravy. Serve the pheasant, shallots and garlic with a little gravy poured over.

ROASTED PHEASANT WITH GARLIC AND SHALLOTS

VENISON CASSEROLE

THIS WINTER CASSEROLE IS SERVED UP DURING THE HUNTING SEASON IN POPULAR GAME AREAS SUCH AS THE ARDENNES, AUVERGNE AND ALSACE. VENISON BENEFITS FROM BEING MARINATED BEFORE COOKING, OTHERWISE IT CAN BE A LITTLE TOUGH.

The easiest way to mix the venison with the marinade is to toss together with your hands.

MARINADE
1/2 onion
4 cloves
8 juniper berries, crushed
8 black peppercorns, crushed
250 ml (1 cup) red wine
1 carrot, roughly chopped
1/2 celery stalk
2 bay leaves
2 garlic cloves
2 pieces lemon zest
5 sprigs of rosemary

1 kg (2 lb 4 oz) venison, cubed
30 g (1 oz) plain (all-purpose) flour
1 tablespoon vegetable oil
1 tablespoon clarified butter
8 French shallots
500 ml (2 cups) brown stock
2 tablespoons redcurrant jelly
sprigs of rosemary

SERVES 4

TO MAKE the marinade, cut the half onion into four pieces and stud each one with a clove. Mix together in a large bowl with the rest of the marinade ingredients. Add the venison, toss well and leave overnight in the fridge to marinate.

LIFT the venison out of the marinade (reserving the marinade), drain and pat dry with paper towels. Season the flour and use to coat the venison (the cleanest way to do this is to put the flour and venison in a plastic bag and toss well).

PREHEAT the oven to 160°C (315°F/Gas 2–3). Heat the oil and clarified butter in a large casserole dish, brown the shallots and then remove from the dish. Brown the venison in the oil and butter, then remove from the casserole.

STRAIN the marinade liquid through a sieve into the casserole and boil, stirring, for 30 seconds to deglaze. Pour in the stock and bring to the boil.

TIP the remaining marinade ingredients out of the sieve onto a piece of muslin and tie up in a parcel to make a bouquet garni. Add to the casserole with the venison. Bring the liquid to simmering point, then put the casserole in the oven. Cook for 45 minutes and then add the shallots. Cook for a further 1 hour.

DISCARD the bouquet garni, remove the venison and shallots from the cooking liquid and keep warm. Add the redcurrant jelly to the liquid and boil on the stovetop for 4–5 minutes to reduce by half. Strain the sauce and pour over the venison. Serve garnished with sprigs of rosemary.

RABBIT FRICASSÉE

THE NAME OF THE DISH COMES FROM AN OLD FRENCH WORD, *FRICASSER*, TO FRY. A FRICASSÉE IS A DISH OF WHITE MEAT, USUALLY CHICKEN, VEAL OR RABBIT, IN A VELOUTÉ SAUCE WITH EGG YOLKS AND CREAM. WILD RABBIT, IF YOU CAN GET IT, HAS A BETTER FLAVOUR THAN FARMED.

60 g (2¹/₄ oz) clarified butter
1 x 1.5 kg (3 lb 5 oz) rabbit, cut into
   8 pieces
200 g (7 oz) button mushrooms
80 ml (¹/₃ cup) white wine
170 ml (²/₃ cup) chicken stock
bouquet garni
80 ml (¹/₃ cup) oil
a small bunch of sage
125 ml (¹/₂ cup) thick
   (double/heavy) cream
2 egg yolks

SERVES 4

HEAT HALF the clarified butter in a large saucepan, season the rabbit and brown in batches, turning once. Remove from the saucepan and set aside. Add the remaining butter to the saucepan and brown the mushrooms.

PUT the rabbit back into the saucepan with the mushrooms. Add the wine and boil for a couple of minutes before adding the stock and bouquet garni. Cover the pan tightly and simmer gently over very low heat for 40 minutes.

MEANWHILE, heat the oil in a small saucepan. Remove the leaves from the bunch of sage and drop them, a few at a time, into the hot oil. The leaves will immediately start to bubble around the edges. Cook them for 30 seconds, or until bright green and crispy. Make sure you don't overheat the oil or cook the leaves for too long or they will turn black and taste burnt. Drain the leaves on paper towels and sprinkle with salt.

LIFT the cooked rabbit and mushrooms out of the saucepan and keep warm. Discard the bouquet garni. Remove the pan from the heat, mix together the cream and egg yolks and stir quickly into the stock. Return to very low heat and cook, stirring, for about 5 minutes to thicken slightly (don't let the sauce boil or the eggs will scramble). Season with salt and pepper.

TO SERVE, pour the sauce over the rabbit and mushrooms and garnish with crispy sage leaves.

While the rabbit is simmering, deep-fry the sage until crispy.

BOEUF BOURGUIGNON

ALMOST EVERY REGION OF FRANCE HAS ITS OWN STYLE OF BEEF STEW, BUT BURGUNDY'S VERSION

IS THE MOST WELL KNOWN. IF YOU CAN, MAKE IT A DAY IN ADVANCE TO LET THE FLAVOURS DEVELOP.

SERVE WITH A SALAD OF ENDIVE, CHICORY AND WATERCRESS AND BREAD OR NEW POTATOES.

If you have time, leave the beef to marinate overnight to deepen the flavours of this dish.

1.5 kg (3 lb 5 oz) beef blade or
  chuck steak
750 ml (3 cups) red wine (preferably
  Burgundy)
3 garlic cloves, crushed
bouquet garni
70 g (2½ oz) butter
1 onion, chopped
1 carrot, chopped
2 tablespoons plain (all-purpose)
  flour
200 g (7 oz) bacon, cut into short
  strips
300 g (10½ oz) French shallots,
  peeled but left whole
200 g (7 oz) small button
  mushrooms

SERVES 6

CUT the meat into 4 cm (1½ inch) cubes and trim away any excess fat. Put the meat, wine, garlic and bouquet garni in a large bowl, cover with plastic wrap and leave in the fridge for at least 3 hours and preferably overnight.

PREHEAT the oven to 160°C (315°F/Gas 2–3). Drain the meat, reserving the marinade and bouquet garni. Dry the meat on paper towels. Heat 30 g (1 oz) of the butter in a large casserole dish. Add the onion, carrot and bouquet garni and cook over low heat, stirring occasionally, for 10 minutes. Remove from the heat.

HEAT 20 g (¾ oz) of the butter in a large frying pan over high heat. Fry the meat in batches for about 5 minutes or until well browned. Add to the casserole dish.

POUR the reserved marinade into the frying pan and boil, stirring, for 30 seconds to deglaze the pan. Remove from the heat. Return the casserole to high heat and sprinkle the meat and vegetables with the flour. Cook, stirring constantly, until the meat is well coated with the flour. Pour in the marinade and stir well. Bring to the boil, stirring constantly, then cover and cook in the oven for 2 hours.

HEAT the remaining butter in the clean frying pan and cook the bacon and shallots, stirring, for 8–10 minutes or until the shallots are softened but not browned. Add the mushrooms and cook, stirring occasionally, for 2–3 minutes or until browned. Drain on paper towels. Add the shallots, bacon and mushrooms to the casserole.

COVER the casserole and return to the oven for 30 minutes, or until the meat is soft and tender. Discard the bouquet garni. Season and skim any fat from the surface before serving.

BEEF CARBONNADE

CARBONNADE A LA FLAMANDE IS, AS THE NAME IMPLIES, A FLEMISH RECIPE, BUT IT IS ALSO TRADITIONAL THROUGHOUT THE NORTH OF FRANCE. CARBONNADE MEANS 'CHARCOAL COOKED' BUT THIS IS, IN FACT, A RICH OVEN-COOKED STEW OF BEEF IN BEER. DELICIOUS WITH JACKET POTATOES.

30 g (1 oz) butter
2–3 tablespoons oil
1 kg (2 lb 4 oz) lean beef rump or
    chuck steak, cubed
4 onions, chopped
1 garlic clove, crushed
1 teaspoon brown sugar
1 tablespoon plain (all-purpose) flour
500 ml (2 cups) beer (bitter or stout)
2 bay leaves
4 sprigs of thyme

CROUTONS
6–8 slices baguette
Dijon mustard

SERVES 4

PREHEAT the oven to 150°C (300°F/Gas 2). Melt the butter in a large sauté pan with a tablespoon of oil. Brown the meat in batches over high heat and then lift out onto a plate.

ADD ANOTHER tablespoon of oil to the pan and add the onion. Cook over moderate heat for 10 minutes, then add the garlic and sugar and cook for a further 5 minutes, adding another tablespoon of oil if necessary. Lift out the onion onto a second plate.

REDUCE the heat to low and pour in any juices that have drained from the browned meat, then stir in the flour. Remove from the heat and stir in the beer, a little at a time (the beer will foam). Return to the heat and let the mixture gently simmer and thicken. Season with salt and pepper.

LAYER the meat and onion in a casserole dish, tucking the bay leaves and sprigs of thyme between the layers and seasoning with salt and black pepper as you go. Pour the liquid over the meat, cover with a lid and cook in the oven for 2¹/₂–3 hours, or until the meat is tender.

TO MAKE the croutons, preheat the grill (broiler). Lightly toast the baguette on both sides, then spread one side with mustard. Arrange on top of the carbonnade, mustard side up, and place the whole casserole under the grill for a minute.

Layer the meat and onion in the dish, adding the herbs and seasoning between the layers, then pour the liquid over the top.

BOEUF EN DAUBE

DAUBES ARE TRADITIONALLY COOKED IN SQUAT EARTHENWARE DISHES CALLED *DAUBIÈRES*, BUT A CAST-IRON CASSEROLE DISH WITH A TIGHT-FITTING LID WILL WORK JUST AS WELL. DAUBES HAIL FROM PROVENCE AND ARE USUALLY SERVED WITH BUTTERED MACARONI OR NEW POTATOES.

The pig's trotter will give a gelatinous texture to the daube, as well as adding extra flavour.

MARINADE
2 cloves
1 onion, cut into quarters
500 ml (2 cups) red wine
2 strips of orange zest
2 garlic cloves
1/2 celery stalk
2 bay leaves
a few parsley stalks

1.5 kg (3 lb 5 oz) beef topside, blade or rump, cut into large pieces
2 tablespoons oil
3 strips pork fat
1 pig's trotter or 225 g (8 oz) piece streaky bacon
750 ml (3 cups) beef stock

SERVES 6

TO MAKE the marinade, push the cloves into a piece of onion and mix together in a large bowl with the remaining marinade ingredients. Season the beef with salt and pepper, add to the marinade and leave to marinate overnight.

HEAT the oil in a saucepan. Lift the beef out of the marinade and pat dry, then brown in batches in the oil and remove to a plate. You might need to use a little of the marinade liquid to deglaze the pan between batches to prevent bits sticking to the bottom of the pan and burning.

STRAIN the marinade through a sieve into a bowl and tip the contents of the sieve into the pan to brown. Remove from the pan. Add the marinade liquid to the pan and boil, stirring, for 30 seconds to deglaze the pan.

PLACE the pork fat in a large casserole, then add the pig's trotter, beef and marinade ingredients. Pour in the marinade liquid and stock. Bring to the boil, then cover, reduce the heat and simmer gently for 2–2 1/2 hours or until the meat is tender.

LIFT the meat out of the casserole into a serving dish, cover and keep warm. Discard the garlic, onion, pork fat and pig's trotter. Pour the liquid through a fine sieve and skim off as much fat as possible, then return to the casserole. Bring to the boil and boil until reduced by half and syrupy. Pour the gravy over the meat to serve.

Speciality award-winning meats for sale at a Paris butcher's shop.

BOEUF A LA FICELLE

THE NAME MEANS SIMPLY 'BEEF ON A STRING', WHICH DESCRIBES THE DISH VERY WELL. THE STRING ALLOWS THE PIECES OF BEEF TO BE LOWERED INTO AND LIFTED OUT OF THE COOKING STOCK. YOU CAN USE THE SAME METHOD TO COOK ONE LARGE PIECE OF BEEF.

1 x 800 g (1lb 12 oz) centre-cut
  beef fillet
875 ml (3¹/₂ cups) beef stock
1 swede (rutabaga), cut into batons
1 carrot, cut into batons
1 celery stalk, cut into batons
2 potatoes, cut into chunks
¹/₄ cabbage, chopped
4 spring onions (scallions), trimmed
  into long lengths
1 bay leaf
2 sprigs of thyme
a few sprigs of parsley

SERVES 4

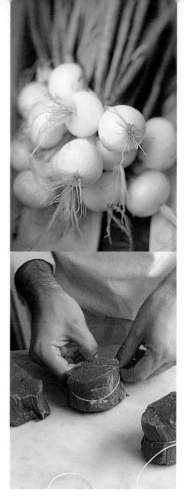

TRIM the beef of any fat and sinew and cut into four even pieces. Tie each piece of beef around its circumference with kitchen string so it keeps its compact shape. Leave a long length of string attached to lower the beef in and out of the stock.

PLACE the stock in a saucepan, bring to the boil and add the vegetables and herbs. Cook over moderate heat for about 8 minutes, or until the vegetables are tender. Lift out the vegetables with a slotted spoon and keep warm. Discard the herbs and skim the stock of any fat or foam that floats to the surface.

SEASON the beef with salt, then lower into the simmering stock, keeping the strings tied around the saucepan handle or a wooden spoon balanced over the pan. Cook for about 6 minutes for rare, or 10 minutes for medium-rare, depending on your tastes.

PLACE each piece of beef in a large shallow bowl and loop the end of the string onto the rim of the bowl. Add the cooked vegetables and ladle some of the cooking broth over the top to serve.

Tie a length of string around each piece of beef. Leave long tails to lower the meat into the stock (tie them round the pan handle while you are cooking).

A Paris butcher delivers fresh meat by scooter.

Press the peppercorns firmly into the steaks, so they don't come off while you are frying.

STEAK BÉARNAISE

STEAK AU POIVRE

4 x 200 g (7 oz) fillet steaks
2 tablespoons oil
6 tablespoons black peppercorns, crushed
40 g (1¹/₂ oz) butter
3 tablespoons Cognac
60 ml (¹/₄ cup) white wine
125 ml (¹/₂ cup) thick (double/heavy) cream

SERVES 4

RUB the steaks on both sides with the oil and press the crushed peppercorns into the meat. Melt the butter in a large frying pan and cook the steaks for 2–4 minutes on each side, depending on how you like your steak.

ADD the Cognac and flambé by lighting the pan with your gas flame or a match (stand well back when you do this and keep a pan lid handy for emergencies). Put the steaks on a hot plate. Add the wine to the pan and boil, stirring, for 1 minute to deglaze the pan. Add the cream and stir for 1–2 minutes. Season and pour over the steaks.

STEAK BÉARNAISE

1 French shallot, finely chopped
2 tablespoons white wine vinegar or tarragon vinegar
2 tablespoons white wine
3 sprigs of tarragon
1 teaspoon dried tarragon
3 egg yolks
200 g (7 oz) clarified butter, melted
1 tablespoon chopped tarragon leaves
4 x 200 g (7 oz) fillet steaks
1 tablespoon oil

SERVES 4

PUT the shallot, vinegar, wine, tarragon sprigs and dried tarragon in a saucepan. Bring to the boil and cook until reduced to 1 tablespoon. Remove from the heat and cool slightly.

WHISK the egg yolks with 1¹/₂ tablespoons water, and add to the saucepan. Place the pan over very low heat or over a simmering bain-marie and continue to whisk until the sauce is thick. Do not boil or the eggs will scramble.

REMOVE the sauce from the heat, continue to whisk and slowly add the butter in a thin steady stream. Pass through a fine strainer, then stir in the chopped tarragon. Season with salt and pepper and keep warm while cooking the steaks.

RUB the steaks with the oil, season them with salt and pepper and cook for 2–4 minutes on each side, depending on how you like your steak. Serve with the sauce.

ENTRECÔTE A LA BORDELAISE

SAUCE

50 g (1³/₄ oz) unsalted butter,
    chilled and diced
3 French shallots, finely chopped
500 ml (2 cups) red wine (preferably
    Bordeaux)
250 ml (1 cup) brown stock
80 g (3 oz) bone marrow
1 tablespoon chopped parsley

4 x 200 g (7 oz) entrecôte or sirloin
    steaks
1¹/₂ tablespoons oil

SERVES 4

TO MAKE the sauce, melt 20 g (³/₄ oz) of the butter in a saucepan, add the shallots and cook, stirring, for 7 minutes or until very soft. Pour in the wine and simmer until reduced by two-thirds. Add the stock and bone marrow and simmer until reduced by half, breaking up the marrow as it cooks.

WHISK IN the remaining pieces of butter. Season to taste with salt and pepper. Add the parsley.

TRIM and season the steaks and rub with some of the oil. Heat the remaining oil in a frying pan, and sauté the steaks for 2–4 minutes on each side, depending on how you like your steak. Pour the sauce over the top to serve.

BIFTECK HACHÉ

BIFTECK HACHÉ MEANS CHOPPED OR MINCED STEAK, OTHERWISE KNOWN AS A HAMBURGER. GOOD

HAMBURGERS NEED TO BE MADE WITH A TENDER MEAT BECAUSE THEY ARE COOKED QUICKLY. ADD

THE SALT JUST BEFORE YOU COOK SO AS NOT TO DRAW THE MOISTURE OUT OF THE MEAT.

Bifteck haché has a better flavour and texture if you use minced steak rather than minced beef.

30 g (1 oz) butter
1 garlic clove, crushed
1 small onion, finely chopped
500 g (1 lb 2 oz) lean beef steak,
    minced
1 tablespoon finely chopped parsley
a large pinch of grated nutmeg
1 large egg, lightly beaten
1 tablespoon oil

SERVES 4

MELT 10 g (¹/₄ oz) of the butter in a saucepan and gently cook the garlic and onion for 10–15 minutes, or until the onion is softened but not browned. Cool.

PUT the minced steak in a large bowl and add the onion mixture, parsley, nutmeg, beaten egg and plenty of ground black pepper. Mix together well, then divide the mixture into four and roll into four balls. Put the balls on a large plate and gently pat each one down into a burger shape. Cover and chill in the fridge for at least 1 hour.

MELT the remaining butter and the oil in a frying pan, slide in the burgers and season with salt. Cook for 10–12 minutes over moderate heat, turning them halfway through. The burgers should be crusty on the outside and slightly pink on the inside. Serve with salad and *frites*.

BIFTECK HACHÉ

BOEUF EN CROÛTE

FOR THIS DISH TO WORK REALLY WELL, YOU NEED TO ASK THE BUTCHER FOR A PIECE OF CENTRE-CUT BEEF FILLET THAT IS AN EVEN THICKNESS ALL THE WAY ALONG. THE PASTRY CAN BE PUFF, FLAKY OR EVEN BRIOCHE DOUGH. BEEF WELLINGTON IS THE ENGLISH EQUIVALENT.

Fold the beef tightly into the pastry parcel as the meat will shrink slightly when cooked.

PÂTÉ
180 g (6 oz) butter
3 French shallots, chopped
1 garlic clove, chopped
360 g (12½ oz) chicken livers
1 tablespoon brandy or Cognac

1 x 1 kg (2 lb 4 oz) thick beef fillet
30 g (1 oz) dripping or butter
1 quantity puff pastry (page 281)
1 egg, lightly beaten

SERVES 6

PREHEAT the oven to 220°C (425°F/Gas 7). To make the pâté, melt half the butter in a frying pan and add the shallots and garlic. Cook until softened but not browned.

REMOVE any discoloured spots from the chicken livers, wash and pat dry. Add the chicken livers to the frying pan and sauté for 4–5 minutes, or until cooked but still a little pink in the middle. Let the livers cool completely and then process in a food processor with the rest of the butter and the brandy. Alternatively, push the chopped livers through a sieve and mix with the butter and brandy. Season.

TIE the beef four or five times along its length to keep it in shape. Heat the dripping in a roasting tin and brown the beef on all sides, then put in the oven and roast for 20 minutes. Allow to cool and remove the string.

REDUCE the oven temperature to 200°C (400°F/Gas 6). Roll the pastry into a rectangle just big enough to cover the beef fillet completely. Trim the edges and keep them for decoration. Spread the pâté over the pastry, leaving a border around the edge. Brush the border with beaten egg.

LAY the fillet on the pastry and wrap it up tightly like a parcel, pressing the seams together firmly and tucking the ends under. Put the parcel, seam side down, on a baking tray and brush all over with beaten egg. Cut pieces from the trimmings to decorate the pastry and brush with beaten egg. Bake for 25–30 minutes for rare and 35–40 minutes for medium. Allow the beef to rest for 5 minutes before carving.

Cattle farming is a major industry of the Alpine areas.

ARTISAN CHARCUTIERS are found selling their products in markets and charcuteries all over France, often made using traditional methods of drying, smoking and cooking. Each region has its own specialities, such as these myrtilles from Provence, and many are not found outside the area and are flavoured with local vegetables, fruits, herbs and spices. Flavourings include garlic, though this is usually used in

CHARCUTERIE

IN FRANCE, ALMOST EVERY VILLAGE HAS A CHARCUTERIE SELLING FRESH AND AIR-DRIED SAUSAGES, HAMS AND PÂTÉS, AND THE ART OF THE ARTISAN CHARCUTIER LIVES ON IN A WEALTH OF SPECIAL LOCAL AND REGIONAL CHARCUTERIE.

Meaning literally 'cured meat', the term charcuterie generally refers to cured or cooked pork products, though other meats can be used, from game and beef in sausages, to goose and duck in foie gras and pâtés. Traditionally horse and donkey meat were also used, but this is increasingly rare. Charcuterie is associated with pork more than any other meat as virtually any part of the pig can be transformed into someting to eat. Pigs have traditionally been kept by rural

families and slaughtered in the autumn, their fresh meat eaten and the rest made into items that could be preseved and eaten through the winter.

Charcuterie is made commercially and by artisan charcutiers all over France. In the Northeast, charcuterie from Alsace has been influenced by Germanic traditions, while the forests of the Ardennes have provided the game, such as wild boar, for hams and pâtes. The Northwest is famous for its rillettes from Tours and Vouvray, and the Southwest for its goose and duck foie gras and Bayonne ham. The East, specifically Lyon, is the acknowledged home of charcuterie and its andouillettes, Jésus, cervelas and rosettes are well known all over France. The South makes good *saucissons secs* and air-dried hams.

SAUCISSES

Saucisses, or fresh sausages, vary from the coarse pork saucisse de Toulouse to the frankfurter-like saucisse de Strasbourg. Boudin noir, a kind of black pudding, and boudin

FOIE GRAS has been a great delicacy since ancient times, and in Castels in Périgord, Marc and Marcelle Boureau continue to produce it in their farm by traditional methods. Their geese are raised in warm barns where they listen to music to calm them (stressed birds do not eat or grow well), and they come outside during the day to feed and wander about. When they are from three to six months old, Marc begins the

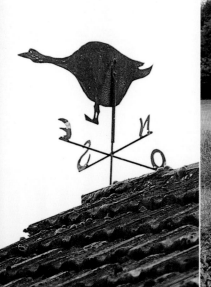

fresh sausages rather than *saucissons secs* as it may turn rancid; caraway seeds (*carvi*), used in the charcuterie of Alsace; *quatre-épices* (cinnamon, pepper, nutmeg and cloves), added to sausages and pâtés; juniper berries (*baies de genièvre*), used to flavour game; sage (*sauge*), mixed with pork; and thyme (*thym*), added to sausages and pâtés, especially rabbit and chicken.

blanc are sausage-like charcuterie, while andouilles and andouillettes are sausages made from chitterlings or tripe. Fresh sausages are often poached rather than grilled (broiled) and these *saucisses à cuire* (boiling sausages), like cervelas, are generally larger and fattier and used in dishes such as a potato salad, *choucroute garnie* or cassoulet.

SAUCISSONS SECS

Saucissons secs, or dried sausages, are like Italian salamis and are usually cured by air-drying. They need no cooking and are sliced and eaten cold. Most are made from pork, though some may include horse meat or beef. Spicing and flavouring varies a lot regionally and much of what is made is only sold locally. Lyon is a great centre for this charcuterie, including rosettes and Jésus, and elsewhere other fine products include pork and beef saucisson d'Arles from Provence; French and German-influenced *saucissons* from Alsace; and rustic, coarse sausages, such as saucisson sec d'Auvergne, from Limousin and the Auvergne.

JAMBON

Hams have been made in France since before the Romans. Jambon de Bayonne is probably the best-known *jambon cru* (raw ham), air-dried and sweet like Parma ham. Alsace and the Ardennes are famous for *jambon cru fumé* (smoked raw hams). Cooked hams are called *jambon* or *jambon cuit*.

PÂTES AND TERRINES

Originally meaning more a 'pie' (now called *pâté en croûte*), pâté now refers only to the filling and is similar to a terrine. Other ready-made items sold by charcuteries include galantines, rillettes and *rillons* (fried pieces of pork belly).

FOIE GRAS AND CONFITS

Fattened duck and goose livers, a speciality of southwest France, are sold on their own or made into parfait (mixed with a little chicken liver) or pâté (made with half pork pâté). Confit is made from pork, duck or goose meat cooked in its own fat and used in *cassoulet* and *garbure,* a hearty cabbage soup.

gavage, feeding them corn by hand through a funnel so that in a few weeks their liver becomes three or four times its normal size. The geese are killed on the farm and the foie gras prepared there, along with confit made from the meat by cooking it slowly in goose fat. Today, *foie gras d'oie* is increasingly rare as more farmers switch to ducks, which are less delicate to raise as well as taking less time to fatten.

PORK NOISETTES WITH PRUNES

PORK WITH PRUNES IS A TYPICAL DISH OF THE ORCHARD-RICH TOURAINE REGION. IT IS SOMETIMES SAID THAT THE FRENCH GENERALLY DO NOT COMBINE FRUIT WITH MEAT, SWEET FLAVOURS WITH SAVOURY, BUT PRUNES AND APPLES ARE BOTH ENTHUSIASTICALLY COMBINED WITH PORK.

8 pork noisettes or 2 x 400 g
  (14 oz) pork fillets
16 prunes, pitted
1 tablespoon oil
50 g (1³/₄ oz) butter
1 onion, finely chopped
150 ml (5¹/₂ fl oz) white wine
280 ml (10 fl oz) chicken or
  brown stock
1 bay leaf
2 sprigs of thyme
250 ml (1 cup) thick (double/heavy)
  cream

SERVES 4

TRIM any excess fat from the pork, making sure you get rid of any membrane that will cause the pork to shrink. If you are using pork fillet, cut each fillet into four diagonal slices. Put the prunes in a small saucepan, cover with cold water and bring to the boil. Reduce the heat and simmer the prunes for 5 minutes. Drain well.

HEAT the oil in a large heavy-based frying pan and add half the butter. When the butter starts foaming, add the pork, in batches if necessary, and sauté on both sides until cooked. Transfer the pork to a warm plate, cover and keep warm.

POUR OFF the excess fat from the pan. Melt the remaining butter, add the onion and cook over low heat until softened but not browned. Add the wine, bring to the boil and simmer for 2 minutes. Add the stock, bay leaf and thyme and bring to the boil. Reduce the heat and simmer for 10 minutes or until reduced by half.

STRAIN the stock into a bowl and rinse the frying pan. Return the stock to the pan, add the cream and prunes and simmer for 8 minutes, or until the sauce thickens slightly. Tip the pork back into the pan and simmer until heated through.

Sauté the pork on both sides, then keep it warm while you make the sauce.

LYONNAIS SAUSAGES

Cervelas often contain pistachio nuts for extra flavour.

50 g (1¾ oz) butter
500 g (1 lb 2 oz) onions, chopped
large pinch of sugar
12 pork sausages with pistachio nuts (*cervelas* or *saucisses à cuire*)
2 tablespoons white wine vinegar
150 ml (5½ fl oz) dry white wine
3 tablespoons finely chopped parsley

SERVES 6

MELT the butter in a large saucepan and add the onion and sugar, stirring to coat the onion in the butter. Cover the pan and cook the onion over low heat for 40–45 minutes, or until caramelized. Preheat the grill (broiler).

PRICK the sausages and poach gently in boiling water for 15 minutes until cooked through. Drain and then grill (broil) until golden brown.

MIX TOGETHER the vinegar and wine. Increase the heat under the caramelized onion and add the vinegar and wine. Allow to bubble for a few minutes until about half of the liquid has evaporated. Stir in the parsley and taste for seasoning. Serve with the sausages.

ANDOUILLETTES

THESE TRIPE SAUSAGES ARE OFTEN BOUGHT READY COOKED AND DO NOT NEED TO BE BOILED. THEY CAN BE FOUND THROUGHOUT FRANCE, ALTHOUGH TYPES DO VARY A LITTLE BETWEEN REGIONS. SOME ARE MADE FROM PIGS' INTESTINES, OTHERS CONTAIN VEAL.

8 andouillettes

SERVES 4

IF YOU have bought andouillettes that are loosely wrapped rather than cased in sausage skins, slash them a couple of times across the top.

PREHEAT the grill (broiler) to moderate heat. Prick the andouillettes all over with a small skewer and arrange them in one layer on a baking tray. Grill (broil) the sausages gently, turning them frequently until they are browned and cooked through. Serve with mashed potatoes or potato gratin and plenty of French mustard.

ANDOUILLETTES

SALT PORK WITH LENTILS

IT IS THOUGHT THAT THE DRY CLIMATE AND VOLCANIC SOIL AROUND THE TOWN OF LE PUY-EN-VELAY

IN THE AUVERGNE ARE THE LUCKY COMBINATION THAT PRODUCES THE REGION'S SUPERIOR GREEN

LENTIL. THEY ARE MORE EXPENSIVE THAN OTHER VARIETIES, BUT HAVE A SUPERB FLAVOUR.

1 kg (2 lb 4 oz) salt pork belly, cut
  into thick strips
1 small salt pork knuckle
1 large carrot, cut into chunks
200 g (7 oz) swede (rutabaga) or
  turnips, peeled and cut into
  chunks
100 g (3 1/2 oz) leek, white part only,
  thickly sliced
1 parsnip, cut into chunks
1 onion, studded with 4 cloves
1 garlic clove
bouquet garni
2 bay leaves
6 juniper berries, slightly crushed
350 g (12 oz) puy lentils
2 tablespoons chopped parsley

SERVES 6

DEPENDING ON the saltiness of the pork you are using, you may need to soak it in cold water for several hours or blanch it before using. Ask your butcher whether to do this.

PUT the pork in a large saucepan with all the ingredients except the lentils and parsley. Stir thoroughly, then add just enough water to cover the ingredients. Bring to the boil, then reduce the heat, cover the pan and leave to simmer gently for 1 1/4 hours.

PUT the lentils in a sieve and rinse under cold running water. Add to the saucepan and stir, then replace the lid and simmer for a further 45–50 minutes, or until the pork and lentils are tender.

DRAIN the pan into a colander, discarding the liquid. Return the contents of the colander to the saucepan, except for the whole onion which can be thrown away. Season the pork and lentils with plenty of black pepper and taste to see if you need any salt. Stir in the parsley.

Use a pan large enough to fit all the ingredients comfortably. Unlike other varieties, puy lentils keep their shape when cooked.

PORK CHOPS WITH BRAISED RED CABBAGE

Braise the red cabbage slowly to bring out the sweetness.

BRAISED RED CABBAGE
30 g (1 oz) clarified butter
1 onion, finely chopped
1 garlic clove, crushed
1 small red cabbage, shredded
1 dessert apple, peeled and sliced
80 ml (1/3 cup) red wine
1 tablespoon red wine vinegar
1/4 teaspoon ground cloves
1 tablespoon finely chopped sage

1 tablespoon clarified butter
4 x 200 g (7 oz) pork chops, trimmed
80 ml (1/3 cup) white wine
410 ml (1²/3 cups) chicken stock
3 tablespoons thick (double/heavy) cream
1 1/2 tablespoons Dijon mustard
4 sage leaves

SERVES 4

TO BRAISE the cabbage, put the clarified butter in a large saucepan, add the onion and garlic and cook until softened but not browned. Add the cabbage, apple, wine, vinegar, cloves and sage and season with salt and pepper. Cover the pan and cook for 30 minutes over very low heat. Uncover the pan and cook, stirring, for a further 5 minutes to evaporate any liquid.

MEANWHILE, heat the clarified butter in a frying pan, season the chops and brown well on both sides. Add the wine and stock, cover and simmer for 20 minutes, or until the pork is tender.

REMOVE the chops from the frying pan and strain the liquid. Return the liquid to the pan, bring to the boil and cook until reduced by two-thirds. Add the cream and mustard and stir over very low heat without allowing to boil, until the sauce has thickened slightly. Pour over the pork chops and garnish with sage. Serve with the red cabbage.

PORK CHOPS WITH CALVADOS

55 g (2 oz) butter
2 dessert apples, cored, each cut into 8 wedges
1/2 teaspoon sugar
1 1/2 tablespoons oil
4 x 200 g (7 oz) pork chops, trimmed
2 tablespoons Calvados
2 French shallots, finely chopped
250 ml (1 cup) dry cider
125 ml (1/2 cup) chicken stock
150 ml (5 1/2 fl oz) thick (double/heavy) cream

SERVES 4

MELT half the butter in a frying pan, add the apple and sprinkle with the sugar. Cook over low heat, turning occasionally, until tender and glazed.

HEAT the oil in a frying pan and sauté the pork chops until cooked, turning once. Pour the excess fat from the pan, add the Calvados and flambé by lighting the pan with your gas flame or a match (stand well back when you do this and keep a pan lid handy for emergencies). Transfer the pork to a plate and keep warm.

ADD the remaining butter to the pan and cook the shallots until soft but not brown. Add the cider, stock and cream and bring to the boil. Reduce the heat and simmer for 15 minutes, or until reduced enough to coat the back of a spoon.

SEASON the sauce, add the pork and simmer for 3 minutes to heat through. Serve with the apple.

PORK CHOPS WITH CALVADOS

BLANQUETTE DE VEAU

BLANQUETTES ARE USUALLY SERVED WITH PLAIN WHITE RICE OR BOILED NEW POTATOES. THEY CAN VARY FROM REGION TO REGION, BUT THIS ONE WITH MUSHROOMS AND ONIONS AND A SAUCE THICKENED WITH CREAM AND EGGS IS A CLASSIC RECIPE.

800 g (1 lb 12 oz) boneless veal shoulder, cut into 3 cm (1¼ inch) cubes
1 litre (4 cups) brown stock
4 cloves
½ large onion
1 small carrot, roughly chopped
1 leek, white part only, roughly chopped
1 celery stalk, roughly chopped
1 bay leaf
30 g (1 oz) butter
30 g (¼ cup) plain (all-purpose) flour
1 tablespoon lemon juice
1 egg yolk
2½ tablespoons thick (double/heavy) cream

ONION GARNISH
250 g (9 oz) pickling or pearl onions
10 g (¼ oz) butter
1 teaspoon caster (superfine) sugar

MUSHROOM GARNISH
10 g (¼ oz) butter
2 teaspoons lemon juice
150 g (5½ oz) button mushrooms, trimmed

SERVES 6

PUT the veal in a large saucepan, cover with cold water and bring to the boil. Drain, rinse well and drain again. Return to the pan and add the stock. Press the cloves into the onion and add to the pan with the remaining vegetables and bay leaf.

BRING to the boil, reduce the heat, cover and simmer for 40–60 minutes, or until the veal is tender. Skim the surface occasionally. Strain, reserving the cooking liquid and throwing away the vegetables. Keep the veal warm.

TO MAKE the onion garnish, put the onions in a small pan with enough water to half cover them. Add the butter and sugar. Place a crumpled piece of greaseproof paper directly over the onions. Bring to a simmer and cook over low heat for 20 minutes, or until the water has evaporated and the onions are tender.

TO MAKE the mushroom garnish, half-fill a small pan with water and bring to the boil. Add the butter, lemon juice and mushrooms and simmer for 3 minutes, or until the mushrooms are tender. Drain the mushrooms, discarding the liquid.

HEAT the butter in a large saucepan. Stir in the flour to make a roux and cook, stirring, for 3 minutes without allowing the roux to brown. Remove from the heat and gradually add the cooking liquid from the veal, stirring after each addition until smooth. Return to the heat and whisk until the sauce comes to the boil, then reduce the heat to low and simmer for 8 minutes, or until the sauce coats the back of the spoon.

ADD the lemon juice and season well. Quickly stir in the egg yolk and cream, then add the veal and the onion and mushroom garnishes. Reheat gently, without boiling, to serve.

Strain the cooking liquid from the veal and then use to give flavour to the velouté sauce.

Weekly markets offer commercial and home-grown produce.

ROAST VEAL STUFFED WITH HAM AND SPINACH

250 g (9 oz) English spinach
2 garlic cloves, crushed
2 tablespoons finely chopped
   parsley
2 teaspoons Dijon mustard
100 g (3¹/₂ oz) ham on the bone,
   diced
finely grated zest of 1 lemon
1 x 600 g (1 lb 5 oz) piece
   boneless veal loin or fillet, beaten
   with a meat mallet to measure
   30 x 15 cm/12 x 6 inches (ask
   your butcher to do this)
4 rashers streaky bacon
2 tablespoons olive oil
50 g (1³/₄ oz) butter
16 baby carrots
8 small potatoes, unpeeled
8 French shallots
185 ml (³/₄ cup) dry (*Sercial*)
   Madeira

SERVES 4

PREHEAT the oven to 170°C (325°F/Gas 3). Wash the spinach and put in a large saucepan with just the water clinging to the leaves. Cover the pan and steam the spinach for 2 minutes or until just wilted. Drain, cool and squeeze dry with your hands. Chop and mix with the garlic, parsley, mustard, ham and lemon zest. Season well.

SPREAD the spinach filling over the centre of the piece of veal. Starting from one of the shorter sides, roll up like a swiss roll. Wrap the rashers of streaky bacon over the meat and season well. Tie with string several times along the roll to secure the bacon and make sure the roll doesn't unravel.

HEAT the olive oil and half the butter in a large frying pan and add the carrots, potatoes and shallots. Briefly brown the vegetables and then tip into a roasting tin. Brown the veal parcel on all sides, then place on top of the vegetables. Add 4 tablespoons of the Madeira to the frying pan and boil, stirring, for 30 seconds to deglaze the pan. Pour over the veal.

ROAST the meat for 30 minutes, then cover the top with foil to prevent overbrowning. Roast for another 45–60 minutes or until the juices run clear when you pierce the thickest part of the meat with a skewer. Wrap the meat in foil and leave to rest. Test the vegetables and return to the oven for a while if they're not yet tender. Remove them from the tin.

PLACE the roasting tin over moderate heat and add the rest of the Madeira. Allow it to bubble, then add the rest of the butter and season the sauce to taste. Slice the veal thickly and arrange the slices of meat on top of the vegetables. Pour over some of the Madeira sauce and serve the rest separately in a jug.

Spread the spinach filling over the piece of veal and then roll up like a swiss roll. Tie with string to keep the bacon rashers in place and prevent the veal unrolling.

VEAL PAUPIETTES

PAUPIETTES ARE SLICES OF MEAT, WRAPPED AROUND A SAVOURY STUFFING AND ROLLED UP TO MAKE LITTLE PARCELS. IN FRANCE, THEY ARE ALSO REFERRED TO AS '*OISEAUX SANS TÊTES*', WHICH MEANS LITERALLY 'BIRDS WITHOUT HEADS'.

STUFFING
30 g (1 oz) butter
2 French shallots, finely chopped
1 garlic clove, crushed
200 g (7 oz) minced (ground) pork
200 g (7 oz) minced (ground) veal
1 egg
2 tablespoons dry white wine
3 tablespoons fresh white
    breadcrumbs
2 tablespoons finely chopped
    parsley

4 x 150 g (5^1/$_2$ oz) veal escalopes,
    pounded flat

SAUCE
30 g (1 oz) clarified butter
1 onion, diced
1 carrot, diced
1 celery stalk, diced
80 ml (^{1}/$_3$ cup) white wine
2 teaspoons tomato paste (purée)
1 bay leaf
330 ml (1^1/$_3$ cups) brown stock

SERVES 4

TO MAKE the stuffing, melt the butter in a small saucepan and cook the shallots over gentle heat until softened but not browned. Add the garlic and cook for a further 2 minutes, then set aside to cool. Mix with the other stuffing ingredients and season with salt and pepper.

LAY the veal escalopes flat and spread evenly with the stuffing, leaving a narrow border around the edge. Roll up the paupiettes, then tie up with string as you would a parcel.

TO MAKE the sauce, melt half the clarified butter in a large sauté pan or frying pan. Add the onion, carrot and celery and soften over low heat. Increase the heat to brown the vegetables, stirring occasionally. Remove from the pan.

HEAT the remaining clarified butter in the sauté pan and brown the paupiettes, turning once. Remove from the pan, pour in the white wine and boil, stirring, for 30 seconds to deglaze the pan. Add the tomato paste and bay leaf. Pour in the stock and bring to a simmer before adding the vegetables and paupiettes.

COVER the pan and cook for 12–15 minutes, or until a skewer poked into the centre of a paupiette comes out too hot to touch. Remove the paupiettes from the pan and keep warm.

STRAIN the sauce, pressing down on the vegetables with a spoon to extract as much liquid as possible. Return the sauce to the pan and boil until reduced by half and syrupy. Slice each paupiette into five pieces and serve with a little sauce poured over the top.

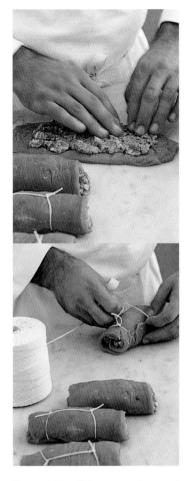

Spread the filling over the veal escalopes, then roll up and tie into parcels with string.

Pavement tables in Paris.

ROAST LEG OF LAMB WITH SPRING VEGETABLES

A POPULAR MEAT IN FRANCE, LAMB COMES IN VARIOUS GUISES. IN SOME AREAS IT FEEDS ON LUSH GRASSLANDS AND, IN OTHERS, ON WILD HERBS. IN NORMANDY, PICARDIE AND BORDEAUX, FLAVOURSOME PRE-SALÉ LAMBS FEED ON SALT MARSHES AND ARE OFTEN SERVED WITHOUT ADDED FLAVOURINGS.

1 x 2 kg (4 lb 8 oz) leg of lamb
3 sprigs of rosemary
6 garlic cloves, unpeeled
500 g (1 lb 2 oz) small potatoes, halved
250 g (9 oz) baby carrots
6 small leeks
250 g (9 oz) small zucchini (courgettes)
1 1/2 tablespoons plain (all-purpose) flour
125 ml (1/2 cup) red wine
170 ml (2/3 cup) brown stock

SERVES 6

PREHEAT the oven to 200°C (400°F/Gas 6). Rub the lamb all over with salt and pepper. Put the lamb in a roasting tin, lay the sprigs of rosemary on top and scatter the garlic around the lamb. Roast for 20 minutes, then turn the lamb over.

ADD the potatoes to the roasting tin and toss in the lamb fat, then return to the oven for a further 15 minutes. Turn the lamb again and cook for another 15 minutes.

ADD the baby carrots and leeks to the tin, toss with the potatoes in the lamb fat and turn the lamb again. Roast for 15 more minutes, then add the zucchini. Toss all the vegetables in the lamb fat and turn the leg of lamb again.

ROAST for another 15 minutes, then lift the lamb out of the roasting tin to rest. The lamb will be rare—if you prefer, cook it for another 5–10 minutes. Remove the vegetables and garlic from the tin and keep warm.

TO MAKE the gravy, spoon the fat from the surface of the meat juices. Place the roasting tin over moderate heat on the stovetop and stir in the flour to make a roux. Cook, stirring, for 2 minutes, then gradually stir in the wine and stock. Boil the gravy for 2 minutes, then strain into a serving jug.

CARVE the lamb and serve with the spring vegetables and garlic. Serve the gravy separately.

Season the lamb generously and roast with just the rosemary and garlic for 20 minutes. Add the vegetables in stages, depending on how long they take to cook.

LAMB BRAISED WITH BEANS

135 g (²/₃ cup) dried haricot beans
1 x 1 kg (2 lb 4 oz) boned shoulder
   of lamb, tied with string to keep
   its shape
30 g (1 oz) clarified butter
2 carrots, diced
2 large onions, chopped
4 garlic cloves, unpeeled
bouquet garni
250 ml (1 cup) dry red wine
250 ml (1 cup) brown stock

SERVES 4

PUT the beans in a large bowl and cover with plenty of water. Leave to soak for 8–12 hours, then drain. Bring a large saucepan of water to the boil, add the beans and return to the boil. Reduce the heat to moderate and cook the beans, partially covered, for 40 minutes. Drain well.

RUB the lamb all over with salt and pepper. Heat the butter over high heat in a large casserole with a tight-fitting lid. Add the lamb and cook for 8–10 minutes, turning every few minutes until well browned. Remove the lamb.

REHEAT the casserole over high heat and add the carrot, onion, garlic and bouquet garni. Reduce the heat and cook, stirring, for 8–10 minutes or until softened. Increase the heat to high and pour in the wine. Boil, stirring, for 30 seconds to deglaze the casserole, then return the lamb to the casserole. Add the stock.

BRING TO the boil, then cover and reduce the heat to low. Braise the meat for 1¹/₂ hours, turning twice. If the lid is not tight fitting, cover the casserole with foil and then put the lid on top.

ADD the cooked beans to the lamb and return to the boil over high heat. Reduce the heat to low, cover the casserole again and cook for a further 30 minutes.

LIFT the lamb out of the casserole, cover and leave to rest for 10 minutes before carving. Discard the bouquet garni. Skim the excess fat from the surface of the sauce and, if the sauce is too thin, boil over high heat for 5 minutes, or until thickened slightly. Taste for seasoning. Carve the lamb and arrange on a platter. Spoon the beans around the lamb and drizzle with the gravy. Serve the rest of the gravy separately.

Use the same casserole to brown the lamb, soften the vegetables and then braise the meat. This will strengthen the flavour of the dish.

A greengrocer at Saint-Rèmy.

Brown the lamb in a couple of batches so that you don't lower the temperature by overcrowding. Once all the meat is browned and coated with flour, slowly stir in the stock.

NAVARIN A LA PRINTANIÈRE

NAVARIN A LA PRINTANIÈRE IS TRADITIONALLY MADE TO WELCOME SPRING AND THE NEW CROP OF YOUNG VEGETABLES. NAVARINS, OR STEWS, CAN ALSO BE MADE ALL YEAR ROUND, USING OLDER WINTER ROOT VEGETABLES SUCH AS POTATOES, CARROTS AND TURNIPS.

1 kg (2 lb 4 oz) lean lamb shoulder
30 g (1 oz) butter
1 onion, chopped
1 garlic clove, crushed
1 tablespoon plain (all-purpose) flour
500 ml (2 cups) brown stock
bouquet garni
18 baby carrots
8 large-bulb spring onions
200 g (7 oz) baby turnips
175 g (6 oz) small potatoes
150 g (5 1/2 oz) peas, fresh or frozen

SERVES 6

TRIM the lamb of any fat and sinew and then cut it into bite-sized pieces. Heat the butter over high heat in a large casserole. Brown the lamb in two or three batches, then remove from the casserole.

ADD the onion to the casserole and cook, stirring occasionally, over moderate heat for 3 minutes or until softened but not browned. Add the garlic and cook for a further minute or until aromatic.

RETURN the meat and any juices to the casserole and sprinkle with the flour. Stir over high heat until the meat is well coated and the liquid is bubbling, then gradually stir in the stock. Add the bouquet garni and bring to the boil. Reduce the heat to low, cover the casserole and cook for 1 1/4 hours.

TRIM the carrots, leaving a little bit of green stalk, and do the same with the spring onions and baby turnips. Cut the potatoes in half if they are large.

ADD the vegetables to the casserole dish, bring to the boil and simmer, covered, for 15 minutes or until the vegetables are tender. (If you are using frozen peas, add them right at the end so they just heat through.) Season with plenty of salt and pepper before serving.

LAMB STUFFED WITH COUSCOUS AND ALMONDS

THE ALMONDS GIVE THIS STUFFING A LOVELY CRUNCHY TEXTURE. WHEN YOU BUY THE MEAT, BE SURE
TO TELL THE BUTCHER YOU ARE INTENDING TO STUFF THE LAMB AND YOU WILL NEED THE HOLE IN
THE MEAT TO BE FAIRLY LARGE. SERVE WITH BOULANGÈRE POTATOES.

80 ml (¹/₃ cup) olive oil
1 small red capsicum (pepper)
1 small yellow capsicum (pepper)
30 g (1 oz) whole blanched
   almonds
1 small onion, chopped
4 garlic cloves
100 g (3¹/₂ oz) eggplant
   (aubergine), diced
400 g (14 oz) tin chopped tomatoes
pinch of sugar
1 tablespoon thyme leaves
2 teaspoons capers, rinsed and
   squeezed dry
8 black olives, pitted and finely
   chopped
50 g (1³/₄ oz) couscous
1 x 1.5 kg (3 lb 5 oz) tunnel-boned
   leg of lamb
¹/₂ small onion

GRAVY
1 tablespoon plain (all-purpose) flour
1 teaspoon tomato paste (purée)
250 ml (1 cup) brown stock
125 ml (¹/₂ cup) red wine

SERVES 6

PREHEAT the oven to 200°C (400°F/Gas 6). Rub
1 tablespoon of oil over the capsicums and roast
for 40–45 minutes, or until blackened. Cool, then
peel the capsicums and cut into long thin strips.

LIGHTLY TOAST the almonds in a dry frying pan,
then chop. Heat 1 tablespoon of oil in the pan and
cook the onion until softened. Crush 2 garlic
cloves, add to the onion and cook for 5 minutes.
Add 2 tablespoons of oil and the eggplant and
cook for 10 minutes. Add the tomato and sugar
and simmer until fairly dry. Remove from the heat
and mix in the thyme, capers and olives. Cool.

POUR 100 ml (3¹/₃ fl oz) boiling water onto the
couscous. Leave for 5 minutes, then fluff the grains
with a fork. Add the couscous, capsicums and
almonds to the eggplant mixture and season well.

INCREASE the oven to 230°C (450°F/Gas 8).
Push as much stuffing as you can into the cavity
of the lamb. (Put any leftover stuffing in an
ovenproof dish.) Fold the meat over the stuffing at
each end and secure with skewers. Put the
remaining cloves of garlic and the half onion in a
roasting tin and place the lamb on top. Roast for
30 minutes, then reduce the oven to 180°C
(350°F/Gas 4) and cook for 1¹/₂ hours (cover with
foil if overbrowning). Bake any extra stuffing for
the last 20 minutes.

TO MAKE the gravy, remove the meat from the
tin, cover and leave to rest. Strain off all but
2 tablespoons of the fat from the tin, then place
over moderate heat. Stir in the flour and tomato
paste and gradually add the stock, stirring. Add
the wine slowly, stirring until the gravy reaches the
consistency you like. Season well. Slice the meat
and serve with the gravy and any extra stuffing.

The couscous and almond filling
should be fairly dry. Pack as
much as you can into the lamb
and cook the rest separately.

CASSOULET

CASSOULET TAKES ITS NAME FROM THE TRADITIONAL CASSEROLE DISH USED FOR COOKING THIS STEW. IT VARIES REGIONALLY IN THE SOUTH OF FRANCE, WITH THE BEST-KNOWN VERSIONS HAILING FROM CARCASSONNE, TOULOUSE AND CASTELNAUDARY.

400 g (2 cups) dried haricot beans
bouquet garni
1/2 large onion, cut into quarters
2 garlic cloves, crushed
225 g (8 oz) salt pork or unsmoked
    bacon, cut into cubes
1 tablespoon clarified butter
400 g (14 oz) lamb shoulder
350 g (12 oz) boiling sausages
    (*saucisses à cuire*)
1 celery stalk, sliced
4 pieces duck confit (page 147) or
    4 pieces roasted duck
6 large tomatoes
180 g (6 oz) Toulouse sausage
4 slices baguette, made into
    crumbs

SERVES 6

PUT the beans in a bowl and cover with cold water. Soak overnight, then drain and rinse.

PUT the beans in a large saucepan with the bouquet garni, onion, garlic and salt pork. Add 2–3 litres (8–12 cups) of cold water, bring to the boil and then simmer for 1 hour.

HEAT the clarified butter in a frying pan. Cut the lamb into eight pieces and brown in the butter. Add the lamb, boiling sausage, celery and duck confit to the top of the beans and push into the liquid. Score a cross in the top of each tomato, plunge into boiling water for 20 seconds, then peel the skin away from the cross. Chop the tomatoes finely, discarding the cores, and add to the top of the cassoulet. Push into the liquid and cook for a further hour.

BROWN the Toulouse sausage in the frying pan and add to the top of the cassoulet. Push into the liquid and cook for 30 minutes more. Preheat the oven to 160°C (315°F/Gas 2–3).

DISCARD the bouquet garni. Strain the liquid into a saucepan and boil over moderate heat until reduced by two-thirds. Remove all the meat from the saucepan, slice the sausages and pull the duck meat from the bones. Layer the meat and beans, alternately, in a deep casserole. Pour in the liquid, to come no higher than the top of the beans.

SPRINKLE the cassoulet with the breadcrumbs and bake for 40 minutes. Every 10 minutes, break the breadcrumb crust with the back of a spoon to let a little liquid come through. If the beans look a bit dry, add a little stock or water to the edge of the dish. Serve straight from the casserole.

Cassoulet can be time-consuming to prepare as the different ingredients are cooked separately and then layered in a deep casserole. Liquid is added up to the top of the beans.

POT AU FEU

THE SIMPLICITY OF THIS DISH OF BOILED MEAT AND VEGETABLES MEANS YOU NEED TO USE THE VERY BEST QUALITY INGREDIENTS. REGIONAL RECIPES VARY, BUT POT AU FEU IS USUALLY SERVED WITH THE MEATS SLICED AND THE BROTH IN A SEPARATE BOWL.

1 tablespoon oil
1 celery stalk, roughly chopped
2 carrots, roughly chopped
1/2 onion, roughly chopped
800 g (1 lb 12 oz) beef shank with
    marrowbone
1 x 600 g (1 lb 5 oz) piece beef
    chuck
2 bay leaves
4 sprigs of thyme
a few parsley stalks
10 peppercorns
800 g (1 lb 12 oz) beef short ribs

VEGETABLE GARNISH
1 large celery stalk
350 g (12 oz) small potatoes
300 g (10 1/2 oz) baby carrots,
    green tops trimmed
200 g (7 oz) baby turnips
350 g (12 oz) baby leeks

Dijon mustard and coarse sea salt,
    to serve

SERVES 4

HEAT the oil in a heavy-based frying pan and cook the chopped celery, carrot and onion over moderately high heat for 10 minutes, or until browned.

REMOVE the meat from the beef shank and reserve the marrowbone. Tie the beef chuck with string so it looks like a parcel.

PUT 3 litres (12 cups) water in a large saucepan and bring to the boil. Add the browned vegetables, herbs, peppercorns, beef shank meat, ribs, and beef chuck to the pan. Return to the boil and skim off any fat that floats to the surface. Reduce the heat, and simmer for 2–2 1/2 hours, or until the meat is very tender.

GENTLY REMOVE the meat to a clean saucepan and strain the cooking liquid over it. Throw away the vegetables. Season the meat with salt and pepper, add the marrowbone and simmer over moderate heat for about 10 minutes. Remove the marrowbone, gently push the marrow out of the bone and slice into six pieces.

MEANWHILE, to make the vegetable garnish, cut the celery into 5 cm (2 inch) lengths, then cut each piece in half lengthways. Cook the potatoes in salted boiling water for 10 minutes, or until tender to the point of a knife, then drain. Add the celery, carrots, turnips and leeks to the meat and cook for 7 minutes. Add the potatoes and cook for another 3 minutes to heat through.

SLICE the meats and serve with the marrow and vegetables. Serve the broth separately in bowls, accompanied by plenty of mustard and sea salt.

While the pot au feu simmers, skim away the fat and froth that floats to the surface.

CHOUCROUTE GARNIE

SAUERKRAUT (CHOUCROUTE), OR PICKLED CABBAGE, IS AN IMPORTANT INGREDIENT IN ALSACE CUISINE. THIS DISH CAN VARY ACCORDING TO THE NUMBER OF PEOPLE YOU WANT TO FEED— TRADITIONALLY, THE MORE PEOPLE THERE ARE, THE WIDER THE VARIETY OF MEAT USED.

Place the ham knuckle on top of the sauerkraut and add the other flavourings, then layer with the rest of the onion, sauerkraut and pork shoulder and belly.

1.25 kg (2 lb 12 oz) fresh or tinned sauerkraut
4 tablespoons bacon fat or lard
1 onion, chopped
1 large garlic clove, crushed
1 onion, studded with 4 cloves
1 ham knuckle or hock
2 bay leaves
2 carrots, diced
8 juniper berries, lightly crushed
1 x 450 g (1 lb) piece pork shoulder
450 g (1 lb) salt pork belly, cut into thick strips
185 ml (³/₄ cup) dry wine, preferably Riesling
12 small potatoes, unpeeled
3 boiling sausages (*saucisses à cuire*)
6 frankfurters

SERVES 8

PREHEAT the oven to 190°C (375°F/Gas 5). If you are using fresh sauerkraut, wash it under cold running water, then squeeze dry. If you are using a tin or jar of sauerkraut, simply drain it well.

MELT the fat or lard in a large casserole, add the chopped onion and garlic and cook for 10 minutes, or until softened but not browned. Remove half the onion from the casserole and keep on one side. Add half the sauerkraut to the casserole, then place the whole onion and the ham knuckle on the sauerkraut. Scatter with the bay leaves, carrot and juniper berries. Season.

NOW ADD the rest of the onion and the remaining sauerkraut and season again. Place the pork shoulder and strips of pork belly on top and pour in the wine and 125 ml (¹/₂ cup) water. Cook, covered, in the oven for 2¹/₂ hours (check after an hour and add a little more water if necessary). Add the whole potatoes and cook for a further 30–40 minutes, or until the potatoes are tender.

POACH the boiling sausages in simmering water for 20 minutes, then add the frankfurters and poach for 10 minutes longer. Drain and keep warm. Discard the studded onion from the casserole. Cut any meat from the ham knuckle or hock and slice the pork shoulder and sausages.

TO SERVE, arrange the piping hot sauerkraut on a large dish with the potatoes, sausages and pieces of meat.

SAUTÉED CALF'S LIVER

4 bacon rashers, cut in half
4 x 150 g (5½ oz) slices calf's liver
90 g (¾ cup) plain (all-purpose)
   flour
1 tablespoon butter

SERVES 4

HEAT a frying pan and cook the bacon until browned and crisp all over. Lift out with a slotted spoon and keep warm. Don't clean the pan.

PEEL OFF any membrane from the liver and cut out any veins with a sharp knife. Season the flour with salt and black pepper, then spread out on a small tray or board. Coat the liver in the flour and shake away the excess.

HEAT the butter in the frying pan with the bacon fat. When the butter is foaming, add the liver and cook for 90 seconds on each side (the liver should still be pink in the middle). Serve the liver and bacon with mashed potatoes.

BOUDIN NOIR WITH APPLES

THERE ARE SEVERAL VARIETIES OF BOUDIN NOIR AVAILABLE IN FRANCE. RECIPES VARY REGIONALLY AND CAN INCLUDE INGREDIENTS SUCH AS APPLES, CREAM AND CHESTNUTS. ENGLISH BLACK PUDDING CAN ALSO BE USED FOR THIS RECIPE.

2 boudin noir or black puddings
2 dessert apples
25 g (1 oz) butter
1 teaspoon soft brown sugar

SERVES 4

CUT the boudin noir into 1 cm (½ inch) slices. Peel and core the apples, cut them into quarters and then into thick slices. Heat the butter in a frying pan and fry the boudin noir on both sides until browned and warmed through. Remove from the pan and keep warm.

FRY the apple in the same pan over high heat, sprinkling it with the brown sugar to help it caramelize. When it is browned on both sides, place on a serving plate and arrange the boudin noir on top. Serve with fried potatoes.

Fry the boudin noir, then keep warm while you caramelize the apples in the same pan.

BOUDIN NOIR WITH APPLES

Use the same frying pan for browning all the ingredients separately. Once you have made the sauce, return the kidneys and chipolatas to the pan.

KIDNEYS TURBIGO

THIS STEW OF KIDNEYS, SAUSAGES AND ONIONS IS NAMED AFTER THE TOWN OF TURBIGO IN LOMBARDY, THE SITE OF TWO FAMOUS FRENCH MILITARY VICTORIES OVER THE AUSTRIAN ARMY IN THE NINETEENTH CENTURY.

8 lamb's kidneys
60 g (2^1/$_4$ oz) butter
8 chipolata sausages
12 small pickling or pearl onions or
  French shallots
125 g (4^1/$_2$ oz) button mushrooms,
  sliced
1 tablespoon plain (all-purpose) flour
2 tablespoons dry sherry
2 teaspoons tomato paste (purée)
250 ml (1 cup) beef stock
2 tablespoons finely chopped
  parsley

CROUTES
oil, for brushing
2 garlic cloves, crushed
12 slices baguette, cut on an angle

SERVES 4

TRIM, HALVE and cut the white membrane from the kidneys with scissors. Heat half the butter in a large frying pan and cook the kidneys for 2 minutes to brown all over. Remove to a plate. Add the chipolatas to the frying pan and cook for 2 minutes until browned all over. Remove to a plate. Cut in half on the diagonal.

LOWER the heat and add the remaining butter to the frying pan. Cook the onions and mushrooms, stirring, for 5 minutes until soft and golden brown.

MIX TOGETHER the flour and sherry to make a smooth paste. Add the tomato paste and stock and mix until smooth.

REMOVE the frying pan from the heat and stir in the stock mixture. Return to the heat and stir until boiling and slightly thickened. Season well with salt and pepper. Return the kidneys and chipolatas to the sauce. Lower the heat, cover the pan and simmer for 25 minutes, or until the kidneys are cooked. Stir occasionally.

MEANWHILE, to make the croutes, preheat the oven to 180°C (350°F/Gas 4). Mix together the oil and garlic and brush over the bread slices. Place on a baking tray and bake for 3–4 minutes. Turn over and bake for a further 3 minutes until golden brown. Sprinkle the kidneys with parsley and serve with the croutes on one side.

VEGETABLES

A vegetable stall in Lyon market.

Crème fraîche is regularly used in place of cream in French kitchens.

PURÉE OF SWEDES

IT IS EASIEST TO MAKE VEGETABLE PURÉES IN A FOOD PROCESSOR OR BLENDER BUT, IF YOU DON'T HAVE ONE, MASH THEM WITH A POTATO MASHER OR USE A FOODMILL. NEVER PURÉE POTATOES IN A PROCESSOR OR BLENDER—THEY BECOME GLUEY.

1 kg swedes (rutabagas), peeled and chopped
2¹/₂ tablespoons butter
1 tablespoon crème fraîche

SERVES 4

PUT the swede in a saucepan, half-cover with water and add 1 teaspoon salt and 1 tablespoon of the butter. Bring to the boil and then reduce the heat, cover, and simmer for 30 minutes or until tender. Drain, reserving the cooking liquid.

PROCESS the swede in a food processor or blender with enough of the cooking liquid to make a purée. Spoon into a saucepan and stir in the remaining butter and the crème fraîche. Reheat gently for a couple of minutes, stirring all the time.

PURÉE OF JERUSALEM ARTICHOKES

750 g (1 lb 10 oz) Jerusalem artichokes, peeled
250 g (9 oz) potatoes, halved
1 tablespoon butter
2 tablespoons crème fraîche

SERVES 4

COOK the artichokes in boiling salted water for 20 minutes or until tender. Drain and then mix in a food processor or blender to purée.

COOK the potatoes in boiling salted water for 20 minutes, then drain and mash. Add to the artichoke with the butter and crème fraîche. Season, beat well and serve at once.

PURÉE OF SPINACH

1 kg (2 lb 4 oz) English spinach
2¹/₂ tablespoons butter, cubed
4 tablespoons crème fraîche
¹/₂ teaspoon nutmeg

SERVES 4

WASH the spinach and put in a large saucepan with just the water clinging to the leaves. Cover the pan and steam the spinach for 2 minutes, or until just wilted. Drain, cool and squeeze dry with your hands. Finely chop.

PUT the spinach in a small saucepan and gently heat through. Increase the heat and gradually add the butter, stirring all the time. Add the crème fraîche and stir into the spinach until it is glossy. Season well and stir in the nutmeg.

PURÉE OF SPINACH

STUFFED GREEN CABBAGE

CHOU FARCI IS A TRADITIONAL DISH FROM THE COOLER REGIONS OF FRANCE—THE CABBAGE CAN COPE WITH A HARSHER CLIMATE THAN MANY OTHER VEGETABLES AND IN THIS DISH IT IS PADDED OUT WITH MEAT TO MAKE A FILLING MAIN COURSE.

The neater that you are able to fill and layer the cabbage leaves, the more regular the shape of the finished dish will be.

STUFFING

4 ripe tomatoes
50 g (1/3 cup) pine nuts
500 g (1 lb 2 oz) pork sausagemeat
150 g (5 1/2 oz) streaky bacon, finely chopped
1 onion, finely chopped
2 garlic cloves, crushed
160 g (2 cups) fresh breadcrumbs
2 eggs
1 tablespoon mixed herbs

1 savoy cabbage, or other loose-leafed cabbage
lemon juice

BRAISING LIQUID

30 g (1 oz) butter
2 French shallots, chopped
1 large carrot, chopped
1 celery stalk, chopped
1 potato, diced
80 ml (1/3 cup) medium-dry white wine
250 ml (1 cup) chicken stock

SERVES 6

TO MAKE the stuffing, score a cross in the top of each tomato, plunge into boiling water for 20 seconds and then peel the skin away from the cross. Chop finely, discarding the cores. Toast the pine nuts under a hot grill (broiler) for 2–3 minutes until lightly browned. Mix together all the stuffing ingredients and season with salt and pepper.

CAREFULLY separate the leaves of the cabbage, trying not to tear them. Save the cabbage heart for use later. Bring a large pan of water to the boil, add a little lemon juice and blanch the cabbage leaves a few at a time. Refresh in cold water, then drain.

SPREAD OUT a damp tea towel on the work surface. Place the four largest leaves in a circle on the cloth with the stems meeting in the middle and the leaves overlapping each other slightly. Spread some of the stuffing over the leaves as evenly as you can.

ARRANGE ANOTHER four cabbage leaves on top and spread with more stuffing. Continue with the rest of the leaves and stuffing, finishing with the smallest leaves. Bring the sides of the tea towel up to meet each other, wrapping the cabbage in its original shape. Tie into a ball with string.

TO MAKE the braising liquid, melt the butter in a large casserole or saucepan and sauté the chopped vegetables for a couple of minutes. Add the wine and boil for 2 minutes, then add the stock. Lower the cabbage into the liquid and cover tightly. Simmer for 1 1/4 hours, or until a metal skewer comes out too hot to touch when poked into the centre of the cabbage. Lift out, unwrap and drain on a wire rack for 5 minutes.

TO SERVE, place some of the braising vegetables and liquid into shallow serving bowls and top with a wedge of stuffed cabbage.

Floury potatoes will soak up the
liquid in the gratin dauphinois
and give a softer, fluffy texture.

GRATIN DAUPHINOIS

POMMES ANNA

850 g (1 lb 14 oz) waxy potatoes
125 g (4¹/₂ oz) clarified butter,
    melted

SERVES 4

PREHEAT the oven to 210°C (415°F/Gas 6–7).
Grease a deep 20 cm (8 inch) round cake tin or
ovenproof dish with melted butter.

PEEL the potatoes and cut into very thin slices
with a mandolin or sharp knife. Lay the potato
slices on paper towels and pat dry. Starting from
the centre of the dish, overlap one-fifth of the
potato slices over the base. Drizzle one-fifth of the
butter over the top. Season well.

REPEAT the layers four more times, drizzling the
last bit of butter over the top. Cut a circle of
greaseproof paper to fit over the top of the
potato. Bake for about 1 hour, or until cooked and
golden and a knife blade slides easily into the
centre. Remove from the oven and leave for
5 minutes, then pour off any excess butter. Run a
knife around the edge to loosen, then turn out
onto a serving plate.

GRATIN DAUPHINOIS

THERE ARE A NUMBER OF VERSIONS OF THIS REGIONAL DISH FROM DAUPHINÉ, SOME WITHOUT THE
TOPPING OF CHEESE. IN FACT, THE WORD GRATIN ORIGINALLY REFERRED NOT TO THE TOPPING, BUT
TO THE CRISPY BITS AT THE BOTTOM OF THE PAN.

1 kg (2 lb 4 oz) floury potatoes
2 garlic cloves, crushed
65 g (¹/₂ cup) grated Gruyère
    cheese
pinch of nutmeg
315 ml (1¹/₄ cups) thick
    (double/heavy) cream
125 ml (¹/₂ cup) milk

SERVES 6

PREHEAT the oven to 170°C (325°F/Gas 3).
Thinly slice the potatoes with a mandolin or
sharp knife. Butter a 23 x 16 cm (9 x 6¹/₂ inch)
ovenproof dish and layer the potatoes, sprinkling
the garlic, grated cheese, nutmeg and seasoning
between the layers and leaving a bit of cheese for
the top. Pour the cream and milk over the top and
sprinkle with the cheese.

BAKE FOR 50–60 minutes or until the potatoes
are completely cooked and the liquid absorbed. If
the top browns too much, cover loosely with foil.
Leave to rest for 10 minutes before serving.

BOULANGÈRE POTATOES

1 kg (2 lb 4 oz) potatoes
1 large onion
2 tablespoons finely chopped
  parsley
500 ml (2 cups) hot chicken or
  vegetable stock
25 g (1 oz) butter, cubed

SERVES 6

PREHEAT the oven to 180°C (350°F/Gas 4). Thinly slice the potatoes and onion with a mandolin or sharp knife. Build up alternate layers of potato and onion in a 20 x 10 cm (8 x 4 inch) deep dish, sprinkling parsley, salt and plenty of black pepper between each layer. Finish with a layer of potato. Pour the stock over the top and dot with butter.

BAKE, covered with foil, on the middle shelf of the oven for 30 minutes, then remove the foil and lightly press down on the potatoes to keep them submerged in the stock. Bake for another 30 minutes, or until the potatoes are tender and the top golden brown. Serve piping hot.

Pushing the mashed potato through a sieve will ensure that the aligot is smooth.

ALIGOT

THIS SPECIALITY OF THE AUVERGNE REGION IS A POTATO PURÉE BEATEN TOGETHER WITH CANTAL CHEESE TO MAKE A STRETCHY ELASTIC MIXTURE. CANTAL IS A SEMI-HARD SMOOTH CHEESE—USE MILD CHEDDAR IF YOU CAN'T FIND IT.

800 g (1 lb 12 oz) floury potatoes,
  cut into even-sized pieces
70 g (2¹/₂ oz) butter
2 garlic cloves, crushed
3 tablespoons milk
300 g (10¹/₂ oz) Cantal (or mild
  Cheddar cheese), grated

SERVES 4

COOK the potatoes in boiling salted water for 20–30 minutes, or until tender. Meanwhile, melt the butter in a small saucepan over low heat and add the garlic. Mash the potatoes and then sieve to give a really smooth purée (don't use a food processor or they will become gluey).

RETURN the potato purée to the saucepan over gentle heat and add the garlic butter and milk. Mix together well and then add the cheese, handful by handful. Beat in the cheese—once it has melted the mixture will be stretchy. Season with salt and pepper before serving.

ALIGOT

Saint Cyprien in the Dordogne.

PEAS WITH ONIONS AND LETTUCE

LETTUCE IS OFTEN THOUGHT OF AS PURELY A SALAD GREEN, BUT IN FACT UNTIL THE EIGHTEENTH CENTURY IT WAS MORE USUALLY COOKED THAN RAW, AND IN FRANCE IT IS STILL OFTEN EATEN THIS WAY, PARTICULARLY IN THIS DISH.

50 g (1³/4 oz) butter
16 small pickling onions or French shallots
500 g (1 lb 2 oz) shelled fresh peas
250 g (9 oz) iceberg lettuce heart, finely shredded
2 sprigs of parsley
1 teaspoon caster (superfine) sugar
125 ml (¹/2 cup) chicken stock
1 tablespoon plain (all-purpose) flour

SERVES 6

MELT 30 g (1 oz) of the butter in a large saucepan. Add the onions and cook, stirring, for 1 minute. Add the peas, lettuce, parsley sprigs and sugar.

POUR IN the stock and stir well. Cover the pan and cook over moderately low heat for 15 minutes, stirring a couple of times, until the onions are cooked through. Remove the parsley.

MIX the remaining butter with the flour to make a beurre manié. Add small amounts to the vegetables, stirring until the juices thicken a little. Season well with salt and black pepper.

VICHY CARROTS

500 g (1 lb 2 oz) carrots
¹/2 teaspoon salt
1¹/2 teaspoons sugar
40 g (1¹/2 oz) butter
1¹/2 tablespoons chopped parsley

SERVES 6

SLICE the carrots quite thinly, then put in a deep frying pan. Cover with cold water and add the salt, sugar and butter. Simmer until the water has evaporated. Shake the pan to glaze the carrot, then add the parsley, toss together and serve.

VICHY CARROTS

VEGETABLE TIMBALES

280 g (10 oz) carrots, chopped
280 g (10 oz) watercress, trimmed
280 g (10 oz) red capsicums
  (peppers)
185 ml ($^3/_4$ cup) thick
  (double/heavy) cream
7 egg yolks
pinch of nutmeg

SERVES 4

PREHEAT the oven to 160°C (315°F/Gas 2–3). Steam the carrot until soft. Wash the watercress and put in a saucepan with just the water clinging to the leaves. Cover the pan and steam the watercress for 2 minutes, or until just wilted. Drain, cool and squeeze dry with your hands.

PREHEAT the grill (broiler). Cut the capsicums in half, remove the seeds and membrane and place, skin-side up, under the hot grill until the skin blackens and blisters. Leave to cool before peeling away the skin.

PURÉE EACH vegetable individually in a food processor, adding a third of the cream to the carrot to make a smooth purée. Pour the capsicum purée into a saucepan and stir over moderate heat until thickened. Put each purée in its own bowl to cool, then divide the remaining cream between the capsicum and watercress purées.

STIR 2 egg yolks into each purée. Divide the last yolk between the watercress and capsicum purées. Season with salt, pepper and nutmeg.

GREASE FOUR timbale moulds and divide the carrot purée equally among them. Smooth the surface. Spoon the watercress purée on top and smooth the surface. Top with the capsicum purée. Put the moulds in a roasting tin and pour in hot water to come halfway up the sides of the timbales. Cook in this bain-marie for 1$^1/_4$ hours.

TO SERVE, hold a plate on top of each timbale and then tip it upside down. Give the plate and timbale one sharp shake and the timbale will release itself. Serve with a salad and baguette.

Smooth each layer as you put it in the mould, so the timbale is neat and even when turned out.

FENNEL, TOMATO AND GARLIC GRATIN

1 kg (2 lb 4 oz) fennel bulbs
80 ml (1/3 cup) olive oil
1 large red onion, halved and thinly
    sliced
2 garlic cloves, crushed
500 g (1 lb 2 oz) tomatoes

GRATIN TOPPING
60 g (2¼ oz) white bread, broken
    into coarse crumbs
65 g (²/₃ cup) grated Parmesan
    cheese
2 teaspoons grated lemon zest
1 garlic clove, crushed

SERVES 4

PREHEAT the oven to 200°C (400°F/Gas 6).
Grease a 21 cm (8½ inch) square gratin dish
with melted butter or oil. Cut the fennel in half
lengthways, then slice thinly.

HEAT the oil in a large frying pan. Cook the onion
for 3–4 minutes until softened but not browned.
Add the garlic and cook for 2 minutes. Add the
fennel and cook, stirring frequently, for 7 minutes
until softened and lightly golden brown.

SCORE a cross in the top of each tomato, plunge
into boiling water for 20 seconds and then peel
the skin away from the cross. Chop roughly and
add to the fennel. Cook, stirring frequently, for
5 minutes until the tomato is softened. Season
well and pour into the dish.

TO MAKE the gratin topping, mix together all the
ingredients, sprinkle over the vegetables and bake
for 15 minutes, or until golden brown and crisp.
Serve immediately.

To make the tian, arrange a layer of zucchini (courgettes) in the dish, then top with cheese, the tomato mixture and thyme.

VEGETABLE TIAN

60 ml (¼ cup) olive oil
500 g (1 lb 2 oz) zucchini
    (courgettes), thickly sliced on
    the diagonal
4 garlic cloves, crushed
pinch of nutmeg
650 g (1 lb 7 oz) tomatoes
2 red onions, chopped
60 ml (¼ cup) white wine
25 g (1 oz) chopped flat-leaf (Italian)
    parsley
130 g (1 cup) grated Gruyère
    cheese
a few small sprigs of thyme

SERVES 4

PREHEAT the oven to 180°C (350°F/Gas 4).
Grease a 15 x 25 cm (6 x 10 inch) ovenproof dish
with melted butter or oil. Heat half the oil in a large
frying pan and add the zucchini and half the garlic.
Cook, stirring, over low heat for 8 minutes, or until
just beginning to soften. Season well with salt,
pepper and nutmeg. Spread evenly into the dish.

SCORE a cross in the top of each tomato, plunge
into boiling water for 20 seconds and then peel
the skin away from the cross. Chop roughly. Cook
the onion in the remaining oil over low heat for
5 minutes, stirring often. Add the remaining garlic,
tomato, wine and parsley. Cook, stirring often, for
10 minutes until all the liquid has evaporated.

SPRINKLE the cheese over the zucchini and
spread the tomato mixture over the top. Scatter
with sprigs of thyme and bake for 20 minutes, or
until heated through.

VEGETABLE TIAN

RATATOUILLE

THE NAME RATATOUILLE COMES FROM THE FRENCH WORD FOR 'MIX' AND WAS PREVIOUSLY USED AS
A FAMILIAR TERM FOR ANY STEW. THIS RECIPE FOLLOWS THE TRADITIONAL VERSION, WITH EACH
INGREDIENT BEING FRIED SEPARATELY BEFORE THE FINAL SIMMERING.

4 tomatoes
2 tablespoons olive oil
1 large onion, diced
1 red capsicum (pepper), diced
1 yellow capsicum (pepper), diced
1 eggplant (aubergine), diced
2 zucchini (courgettes), diced
1 teaspoon tomato paste (purée)
$1/2$ teaspoon sugar
1 bay leaf
3 sprigs of thyme
2 sprigs of basil
1 garlic clove, crushed
1 tablespoon chopped parsley

SERVES 4

SCORE a cross in the top of each tomato, plunge
into boiling water for 20 seconds and then peel
the skin away from the cross. Chop roughly.

HEAT the oil in a frying pan. Add the onion and
cook over low heat for 5 minutes. Add the
capsicums and cook, stirring, for 4 minutes.
Remove from the pan and set aside.

FRY the eggplant until lightly browned all over and
then remove from the pan. Fry the zucchini until
browned and then return the onion, capsicums
and eggplant to the pan. Add the tomato paste,
stir well and cook for 2 minutes. Add the tomato,
sugar, bay leaf, thyme and basil, stir well, cover
and cook for 15 minutes. Remove the bay leaf,
thyme and basil.

MIX TOGETHER the garlic and parsley and add to
the ratatouille at the last minute. Stir and serve.

You can braise white witlof or
the purple-tipped variety. Both
should be pale yellow, rather
than green and bitter.

BRAISED WITLOF

8 witlof (chicory/Belgian endive)
   heads
1 tablespoon butter
1 teaspoon brown sugar
2 teaspoons tarragon vinegar
125 ml ($1/2$ cup) chicken stock
2 tablespoons thick (double/heavy)
   cream

SERVES 4

TRIM the ends from the witlof. Melt the butter in a
deep frying pan and fry the witlof briefly on all
sides. Add the sugar, vinegar and chicken stock
and bring to the boil. Reduce the heat to a
simmer and cover the pan.

SIMMER GENTLY for 30 minutes, or until tender,
turning halfway through. Take the lid off the pan
and simmer until nearly all the liquid has
evaporated. Stir in the cream and serve.

BRAISED WITLOF

Olives growing in Provence.

Frying the spring onions and bacon for the dressing of the salade lyonnaise.

SALADE LYONNAISE

SALADE NIÇOISE

THE TERM 'A LA NIÇOISE' REFERS TO DISHES TYPICAL OF NICE AND ITS SURROUNDING AREA THAT CONTAIN TOMATOES, OLIVES, ANCHOVIES AND GARLIC. A DEBATE RAGES OVER WHAT SHOULD FEATURE IN A SALADE NIÇOISE—APART FROM THE EGG, PURISTS PREFER TO USE ONLY RAW INGREDIENTS.

4 waxy potatoes
1 tablespoon olive oil
200 g (7 oz) small green beans
300 g (10½ oz) tinned tuna in oil
150 g (5½ oz) cherry tomatoes
200 g (7 oz) green lettuce leaves
20 black olives, pitted
2 tablespoons capers
3 hard-boiled eggs, cut into wedges
8 anchovies

VINAIGRETTE
1 garlic clove, crushed
1 teaspoon Dijon mustard
2 tablespoons white wine vinegar
1 teaspoon lemon juice
125 ml (½ cup) olive oil

SERVES 4 AS A STARTER

COOK the potatoes in boiling salted water for 15 minutes or until just tender. Drain, cut into small cubes and place in a bowl. Drizzle with the olive oil and toss well. Halve the green beans and cook in boiling salted water for 3 minutes, then drain and refresh under cold water.

TO MAKE the vinaigrette, whisk together the garlic, mustard, vinegar and lemon juice. Add the oil in a thin steady stream, whisking until smooth.

DRAIN the tuna, put in a bowl and separate into large chunks with a fork. Cut the tomatoes in half. Cover the base of a serving dish with the lettuce leaves. Scatter the potatoes, beans, tuna, tomatoes, olives and capers over the leaves, pour the vinaigrette over the top and decorate with the egg and anchovies.

SALADE LYONNAISE

1 garlic clove, cut in half
oil, for shallow-frying
4 slices white bread, crusts removed, cut into 1 cm (½ inch) cubes
60 ml (¼ cup) olive oil
2 spring onions (scallions), chopped
3 bacon rashers, cut into short strips
80 ml (⅓ cup) red wine vinegar
3 teaspoons wholegrain mustard
225 g (8 oz) frisée (endive), lamb's lettuce (corn salad) and dandelion leaves
4 eggs

SERVES 4 AS A STARTER

RUB the cut garlic over the base of a frying pan. Pour oil into the pan to a depth of 1 cm (½ inch) and fry the bread cubes for 1–2 minutes, or until golden. Drain on paper towels. Wipe out the pan.

HEAT the olive oil in the frying pan and cook the spring onion and bacon for 2 minutes. Add the vinegar and mustard and boil for 2 minutes to reduce by a third. Pour over the salad leaves and toss to wilt a little. Arrange on serving plates.

TO POACH the eggs, bring a pan of water to the boil. Crack each egg into a ramekin, reduce the heat and slide the eggs into the simmering water. Poach for 3 minutes, lift out with a slotted spoon and drain on paper towels. Place on the leaves and sprinkle with the croutons. Serve immediately.

SALADE AUX NOIX

4 thin slices baguette
1 garlic clove, cut in half
80 ml (¹/₃ cup) olive oil
1 large crisp green lettuce or a
  selection of mixed lettuce leaves
1 tablespoon walnut oil
1 tablespoon red wine vinegar
1 teaspoon Dijon mustard
60 g (¹/₂ cup) walnuts, broken into
  pieces
140 g (5 oz) streaky bacon, cut into
  small pieces

SERVES 4 AS A STARTER

PREHEAT the grill (broiler) and rub the bread with the cut garlic to give it flavour. Drizzle a little of the olive oil on each side of the bread and then grill (broil) until golden brown. Leave to cool.

TEAR the lettuce leaves into pieces and arrange in a bowl or on a large platter. Mix together the remaining olive oil, walnut oil, vinegar and mustard and season to make a dressing.

PUT the walnuts in a bowl and cover with boiling water. Leave for 1 minute, drain and shake dry.

COOK the bacon in a frying pan until crisp, then lift out of the pan with a slotted spoon and sprinkle over the lettuce. Add the walnuts to the pan and cook for a couple of minutes until browned, then add to the salad. Pour the dressing into the pan and heat through.

POUR the dressing over the salad and toss well. Add the garlic croutons to serve.

Frying the sweetbreads before adding the creamy dressing gives them a crisp outer layer while the centre stays soft.

SWEETBREADS SALAD

225 g (8 oz) sweetbreads (lamb's
  or calf's)
1 batavia lettuce or a selection of
  mixed lettuce leaves
1 tablespoon butter
1 French shallot, finely chopped
2 tablespoons red wine vinegar
1 tablespoon Dijon mustard
80 ml (¹/₃ cup) olive oil
2 tablespoons cream

SERVES 4 AS A STARTER

SOAK the sweetbreads in cold water for 2 hours, changing the water every 30 minutes, or whenever it turns pink. Put the sweetbreads in a saucepan of cold water and bring them to the boil. Simmer for 2 minutes, then drain and refresh under cold water. Pull off any skin and membrane and divide into bite-sized pieces.

TEAR the lettuce leaves into pieces and arrange on a plate. Melt the butter in a frying pan and fry the shallot until tender. Add the sweetbreads and fry until browned and cooked through. Add the vinegar, mustard, oil and cream to the pan and stir well. Spoon over the salad leaves and serve.

SWEETBREADS SALAD

SALADE AU CHÈVRE

50 g (1/2 cup) walnuts, broken into
   pieces
1 teaspoon flaked sea salt
8 slices baguette
1 large garlic clove, cut in half
125 g (41/2 oz) chèvre (goat's milk
   cheese), cut into 8 slices
55 g (2 oz) mesclun (mixed salad
   leaves and herbs)
1 small red onion, thinly sliced

DRESSING
2 tablespoons olive oil
1 tablespoon walnut oil
11/2 tablespoons tarragon vinegar
1 garlic clove, crushed

SERVES 4 AS A STARTER

PREHEAT the grill (broiler) to hot. Put the walnuts in a bowl and cover with boiling water. Leave for 1 minute, then drain and shake dry. Toast under the grill for 3–4 minutes until golden. Sprinkle sea salt over the top, toss lightly and leave to cool.

PUT the baguette under the grill and toast one side until lightly golden. Remove from the heat and rub the toasted side with the cut garlic. Leave for a few minutes to cool and crisp, then turn over and place a slice of chèvre on each one. Grill (broil) for 2–3 minutes, or until the cheese browns.

TO MAKE the dressing, mix together the olive oil, walnut oil, vinegar and garlic and season well.

TOSS the mesclun, onion and toasted walnuts together on a large platter. Arrange the chèvre croutons on top and drizzle with the dressing. Serve while the croutons are still warm.

For the salade au foie gras, cut the foie gras terrine into eight slices. Slice the truffle as finely as you can and place a slice on top of each piece of foie gras.

SALADE AU FOIE GRAS

100 g (31/2 oz) salad potatoes,
   thickly sliced
12 asparagus spears, cut into short
   lengths
1 small black truffle, very thinly
   sliced into at least 8 pieces
125 g (41/2 oz) foie gras terrine,
   sliced into 8 pieces
1 tablespoon butter
55 g (2 oz) mesclun (mixed salad
   leaves and herbs)

DRESSING
2 tablespoons olive oil
1 tablespoon walnut oil
1 tablespoon Armagnac or Cognac
11/2 tablespoons red wine vinegar

SERVES 4 AS A STARTER

SIMMER the potatoes in boiling salted water for 15 minutes until tender. Remove with a slotted spoon, rinse in cold water and cool. Simmer the asparagus in the water for 3–4 minutes until tender. Drain, rinse under cold water and chill.

TO MAKE the dressing, mix together the olive oil, walnut oil, Armagnac and vinegar. Season well.

PLACE a slice of truffle on the centre of each slice of foie gras and press it in gently. Melt the butter in a frying pan, add the foie gras to the pan and brown lightly, turning after 30 seconds. The foie gras becomes quite soft as it heats, so use a spatula to turn and lift it out. Drain on paper towels and keep warm.

PUT the potatoes, asparagus and mesclun in a bowl. Add the dressing and toss lightly. Top with the foie gras, truffle side up, and sprinkle with any leftover truffle slices. Serve at once.

SALADE AU FOIE GRAS

DESSERTS & BAKING

COFFEE CRÉMETS WITH CHOCOLATE SAUCE

DARK CHOCOLATE (ALSO KNOWN AS PLAIN OR BITTERSWEET) IS AVAILABLE WITH DIFFERENT AMOUNTS OF ADDED SUGAR. FOR A REALLY GOOD CHOCOLATE SAUCE, YOU WANT TO USE CHOCOLATE WITH LESS SUGAR AND MORE COCOA SOLIDS (BETWEEN 50 AND 70%).

250 g (9 oz) cream cheese
250 ml (1 cup) thick (double/heavy)
  cream
4 tablespoons very strong coffee
80 g (1/3 cup) caster (superfine)
  sugar

CHOCOLATE SAUCE
100 g (3 1/3 oz) dark chocolate
50 g (1 3/4 oz) unsalted butter

SERVES 4

The crémets are spooned into muslin-lined ramekins to make them easier to turn out.

LINE FOUR 125 ml (1/2 cup) ramekins or heart-shaped moulds with muslin, leaving enough muslin hanging over the side to wrap over the crémet.

BEAT the cream cheese a little until smooth, then whisk in the cream. Add the coffee and sugar and mix together. Spoon into the ramekins and fold the muslin over the top. Refrigerate for at least 1 1/2 hours, then unwrap the muslin and turn the crémets out onto individual plates, carefully peeling the muslin off each one.

TO MAKE the chocolate sauce, gently melt the chocolate in a saucepan with the butter and 4 tablespoons water. Stir well to make a shiny sauce, then let the sauce cool a little. Pour a little chocolate sauce over each crémet.

PEARS IN RED WINE

1 tablespoon arrowroot
1 bottle red wine
110 g (1/2 cup) sugar
1 cinnamon stick
6 cloves
zest of 1 small orange
zest of 1 small lemon
6 large pears (ripe but still firm)

SERVES 6

MIX the arrowroot with 2 tablespoons of the wine and set aside. Heat the remaining wine in a saucepan with the sugar, cinnamon stick, cloves and orange and lemon zest. Simmer gently for a couple of minutes, until the sugar has dissolved.

PEEL the pears, but don't remove the stalks. Put the whole pears in the saucepan of wine, cover and poach gently for 25 minutes or until they are very tender, turning occasionally. Lift out with a slotted spoon and place in a deep serving dish.

STRAIN the wine to remove the cinnamon stick, cloves and zest, then pour the wine back into the saucepan. Stir the arrowroot and add to the hot wine. Simmer gently, stirring now and then, until thickened. Pour over the pears and leave to soak until cold. Serve with cream or crème fraîche.

PEARS IN RED WINE

COFFEE CRÉMETS WITH CHOCOLATE SAUCE

CINNAMON BAVAROIS

THE NAME OF THIS CREAMY DESSERT IS A PECULIARITY OF THE FRENCH LANGUAGE IN THAT IT CAN BE SPELT IN BOTH THE MASCULINE FORM, 'BAVAROIS' (FROM *FROMAGE BAVAROIS*), AND THE FEMININE 'BAVAROISE' (FROM *CRÈME BAVAROISE*). HOWEVER, ITS CONNECTION TO BAVARIA HAS BEEN LOST.

315 ml (1¼ cups) milk
1 teaspoon ground cinnamon
55 g (¼ cup) sugar
3 egg yolks
3 gelatine leaves or 1½ teaspoons powdered gelatine
½ teaspoon vanilla extract
170 ml (⅔ cup) whipping cream
cinnamon, for dusting

SERVES 6

PUT the milk, cinnamon and half the sugar in a saucepan and bring to the boil. Whisk the egg yolks and remaining sugar until light and fluffy. Whisk the boiling milk into the yolks, then pour back into the saucepan and cook, stirring, until it is thick enough to coat the back of a wooden spoon. Do not let it boil or the custard will split.

SOAK the gelatine in cold water until soft, drain and add to the hot custard with the vanilla. If using powdered gelatine, sprinkle it on the hot custard, leave it to sponge for a minute, then stir it in. Strain the custard into a clean bowl and cool. Whip the cream, fold into the custard and pour into six 125 ml (½ cup) oiled bavarois moulds. Set in the fridge.

UNMOULD by holding the mould in a hot cloth and inverting it onto a plate with a quick shake. Dust with the extra cinnamon.

Drape the warm tuiles over a rolling pin so that they set in a curved shape.

TUILES

2 egg whites
55 g (¼ cup) caster (superfine) sugar
15 g (½ oz) plain (all-purpose) flour
55 g (½ cup) ground almonds
2 teaspoons peanut oil

MAKES 12

BEAT the egg whites in a clean dry bowl until slightly frothy. Mix in the sugar, then the flour, ground almonds and oil. Preheat the oven to 200°C (400°F/Gas 6).

LINE a baking tray with baking paper. Place one heaped teaspoon of mixture on the tray and use the back of the spoon to spread it into a thin round. Cover the tray with tuiles, leaving 2 cm (¾ inch) between them for spreading during cooking.

BAKE for 5–6 minutes or until lightly golden. Lift the tuiles off the tray with a metal spatula and drape over a rolling pin while still warm to make them curl (you can use bottles and glasses as well). Cool while you cook the rest of the tuiles. Serve with ice creams and other creamy desserts.

TUILES

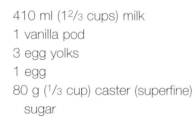

CHOCOLATE MOUSSE

300 g (10¹/₂ oz) dark chocolate,
  chopped
30 g (1 oz) unsalted butter
2 eggs, lightly beaten
3 tablespoons Cognac
4 egg whites
5 tablespoons caster (superfine)
  sugar
500 ml (2 cups) whipping cream

SERVES 8

PUT the chocolate in a heatproof bowl over a saucepan of simmering water, making sure the base of the bowl isn't touching the water. Leave the chocolate until it looks soft and then stir until melted. Add the butter and stir until melted. Remove the bowl from the saucepan and cool for a few minutes. Add the eggs and Cognac and stir.

USING an electric mixer or balloon whisk, beat the egg whites in a clean dry bowl until soft peaks form, adding the sugar gradually. Whisk one-third of the egg white into the chocolate mixture to loosen it and then fold in the remainder with a large metal spoon or spatula.

WHIP the cream and fold into the mousse. Pour into glasses or a large bowl, cover and refrigerate for at least 4 hours.

PETITS POTS DE CRÈME

THE FLAVOUR OF THESE PETITS POTS COMES FROM THE VANILLA POD USED TO INFUSE THE MILK. FOR CHOCOLATE POTS, ADD A TABLESPOON OF COCOA AND 55 GRAMS (2 OZ) MELTED DARK CHOCOLATE TO THE MILK INSTEAD OF THE VANILLA. FOR COFFEE POTS, ADD A TABLESPOON OF GRANULATED COFFEE.

410 ml (1²/₃ cups) milk
1 vanilla pod
3 egg yolks
1 egg
80 g (¹/₃ cup) caster (superfine)
  sugar

SERVES 4

PREHEAT the oven to 140°C (275°F/Gas 1). Put the milk in a saucepan. Split the vanilla pod in two, scrape out the seeds and add the whole lot to the milk. Bring the milk just to the boil.

MEANWHILE, mix together the egg yolks, egg and sugar. Strain the boiling milk over the egg mixture and stir well. Skim off the surface to remove any foam.

LADLE INTO four 25 ml (1 fl oz) ramekins and place in a roasting tin. Pour enough hot water into the tin to come halfway up the sides of the ramekins. Bake for 30 minutes, or until the custards are firm to the touch. Leave the ramekins on a wire rack to cool, then refrigerate until ready to serve.

PETITS POTS DE CRÈME

CHOCOLATE SOUFFLÉS

SOUFFLÉS ARE RENOWNED FOR THEIR DIFFICULTY TO MAKE, BUT CAN IN FACT BE VERY EASY. IF YOU ARE FEELING PARTICULARLY DECADENT WHEN YOU SERVE THESE CHOCOLATE SOUFFLÉS, MAKE A HOLE IN THE TOP OF EACH ONE AND POUR IN A LITTLE CREAM.

40 g (1½ oz) unsalted butter, softened
170 g (¾ cup) caster (superfine) sugar

SOUFFLÉS
1 quantity crème pâtissière (page 285)
90 g (¾ cup) unsweetened cocoa powder
3 tablespoons chocolate or coffee liqueur
85 g (3 oz) dark chocolate, chopped
12 egg whites
3 tablespoons caster (superfine) sugar
icing (confectioners') sugar

SERVES 8

TO PREPARE the dishes, brush the insides of eight 315 ml (1¼ cup) soufflé dishes with the softened butter. Pour a little caster sugar into each one, turn the dishes round to coat thoroughly and then tip out any excess sugar. Preheat the oven to 190°C (375°F/Gas 5) and put a large baking tray in the oven to heat up.

WARM the crème pâtissière in a bowl over a saucepan of simmering water, then remove from the heat. Whisk the cocoa powder, chocolate liqueur and chocolate into the crème pâtissière.

BEAT the egg whites in a clean dry bowl until firm peaks form. Whisk in the sugar gradually to make a stiff glossy mixture. Whisk half the egg white into the crème pâtissière to loosen it, and then fold in the remainder with a large metal spoon or spatula. Pour into the soufflé dishes and run your thumb around the inside rim of each dish, about 2 cm (¾ inch) into the soufflé mixture to help the soufflés rise without sticking.

PUT the dishes on the hot baking tray and bake for 15–18 minutes, or until the soufflés are well risen and wobble slightly when tapped. Test with a skewer through a crack in the side of a soufflé—the skewer should come out clean or slightly moist. If it is slightly moist, by the time you get the soufflés to the table, they will be cooked in the centre. Serve immediately, dusted with a little icing sugar.

Beat egg whites in a clean dry bowl—any hint of grease will prevent them aerating.

RASPBERRY SOUFFLÉ

THERE IS SOMETIMES CONFUSION ABOUT THE DIFFERENCE BETWEEN A SOUFFLÉ AND A MOUSSE. TECHNICALLY, A SOUFFLÉ IS HOT AND A MOUSSE IS COLD. A MOUSSE IS HELD UP BY GELATINE AND EGG WHITE AND WON'T COLLAPSE LIKE A HOT SOUFFLÉ, WHICH IS HELD UP BY HOT AIR.

When adding beaten egg white to a mixture, whisk in a small amount first to loosen it. This allows you to fold in the rest without losing the volume.

40 g (1¹/₂ oz) unsalted butter, softened
170 g (³/₄ cup) caster (superfine) sugar

SOUFFLÉ
¹/₂ quantity crème pâtissière (page 285)
400 g (14 oz) raspberries
3 tablespoons caster (superfine) sugar
8 egg whites
icing (confectioners') sugar

SERVES 6

TO PREPARE the soufflé dish, brush the inside of a 1.5 litre (6 cup) soufflé dish with the softened butter. Pour in the caster sugar, turn the dish round to coat thoroughly and then tip out any excess sugar. Preheat the oven to 190°C (375°F/Gas 5) and put a baking tray in the oven to heat up.

WARM the crème pâtissière in a bowl over a saucepan of simmering water, then remove from the heat. Put the raspberries and half the sugar in a blender or food processor and mix until puréed (or mix by hand). Pass through a fine nylon sieve to get rid of the seeds. Add the crème pâtissière to the raspberries and whisk together.

BEAT the egg whites in a clean dry bowl until firm peaks form. Whisk in the remaining sugar gradually to make a stiff glossy mixture. Whisk half the egg white into the raspberry mixture to loosen it and then fold in the remainder with a large metal spoon or spatula. Pour into the soufflé dish and run your thumb around the inside rim of the dish, about 2 cm (³/₄ inch) into the soufflé mixture, to help the soufflé rise without sticking.

PUT the dish on the hot baking tray and bake for 10–12 minutes, or until the soufflé is well risen and wobbles slightly when tapped. Test with a skewer through a crack in the side of the soufflé—the skewer should come out clean or slightly moist. If it is slightly moist, by the time you get the soufflé to the table, it will be cooked in the centre. Serve immediately, dusted with a little icing sugar.

CHERRY CLAFOUTIS

IT IS TRADITIONAL TO LEAVE THE STONES IN THE CHERRIES WHEN YOU MAKE A CLAFOUTIS (THEY ADD A BITTER ALMOST-ALMOND FLAVOUR DURING THE COOKING), BUT YOU'D BETTER POINT THIS OUT WHEN YOU'RE SERVING THE PUDDING.

185 ml (³/4 cup) thick
  (double/heavy) cream
1 vanilla pod
125 ml (¹/2 cup) milk
3 eggs
55 g (¹/4 cup) caster (superfine) sugar
85 g (²/3 cup) plain (all-purpose) flour
1 tablespoon kirsch
450 g (1 lb) black cherries
icing (confectioners') sugar

SERVES 6

PREHEAT the oven to 180°C (350°F/Gas 4). Put the cream in a small saucepan. Split the vanilla pod in two, scrape out the seeds and add the whole lot to the cream. Heat gently for a couple of minutes, then remove from the heat, add the milk and cool. Strain to remove the vanilla pod.

WHISK the eggs with the sugar and flour, then stir into the cream. Add the kirsch and cherries and stir well. Pour into a 23 cm (9 inch) round baking dish and bake for 30–35 minutes, or until golden on top. Dust with icing sugar and serve.

Adding the unpitted cherries to the clafoutis batter.

PEACHES CARDINAL

4 large ripe peaches
300 g (10¹/2 oz) raspberries
2 dessertspoons icing
  (confectioners') sugar, plus
  extra for dusting

SERVES 4

IF the peaches are very ripe, put them in a bowl and pour boiling water over them. Leave for a minute, then drain and carefully peel away the skin. If the fruit you have is not so ripe, dissolve 2 tablespoons sugar in a saucepan of water, add the peaches and cover the pan. Gently poach the peaches for 5–10 minutes, or until they are tender. Drain and peel.

LET the peaches cool and then halve each one and remove the stone. Put two halves in each serving glass. Put the raspberries in a food processor or blender and mix until puréed (or mix by hand). Pass through a fine nylon sieve to get rid of the seeds.

SIFT the icing sugar over the raspberry purée and stir in. Drizzle the purée over the peaches, cover and chill thoroughly. Dust a little icing sugar over the top to serve.

PEACHES CARDINAL

Dairy cows in Normandy.

Ladling the crème brûlée custard into the ramekins.

CRÈME CARAMEL

CARAMEL
115 g (1/2 cup) caster (superfine) sugar

625 ml (2 1/2 cups) milk
1 vanilla pod
125 g (1/2 cup) caster (superfine) sugar
3 eggs, beaten
3 egg yolks

SERVES 6

TO MAKE the caramel, put the sugar in a heavy-based saucepan and heat until it dissolves and starts to caramelize—tip the saucepan from side to side to keep the colouring even. Remove from the heat and carefully add 2 tablespoons water to stop the cooking process. Pour into six 125 ml (1/2 cup) ramekins and leave to cool.

PREHEAT the oven to 180°C (350°F/Gas 4). Put the milk and vanilla pod in a saucepan and bring just to the boil. Mix together the sugar, eggs and egg yolks. Strain the boiling milk over the egg mixture and stir well. Ladle into the ramekins and place in a roasting tin. Pour enough hot water into the tin to come halfway up the sides of the ramekins. Cook for 35–40 minutes, or until firm to the touch. Remove from the tin and leave for 15 minutes. Unmould onto plates and pour on any leftover caramel.

CRÈME BRÛLÉE

CRÈME BRÛLÉE HAS BEEN KNOWN IN ENGLAND SINCE THE SEVENTEENTH CENTURY BY THE NAME 'BURNT CREAM'. THE CREAMY CUSTARD IS SIMILAR TO THAT OF THE CRÈME CARAMEL, BUT THE TOPPING IS CARAMELIZED TO A HARD CRUST.

CRÈME BRÛLÉE

500 ml (2 cups) cream
185 ml (3/4 cup) milk
115 g (1/2 cup) caster (superfine) sugar
1 vanilla pod
5 egg yolks
1 egg white
1 tablespoon orange flower water
110 g (1/2 cup) demerara sugar

SERVES 8

PREHEAT the oven to 120°C (230°F/Gas 1). Put the cream, milk and half the sugar in a saucepan with the vanilla pod. Bring just to the boil.

MEANWHILE, mix together the remaining sugar, egg yolks and white. Strain the boiling milk over the egg mixture, whisking well. Stir in the orange flower water.

LADLE INTO eight 125 ml (1/2 cup) ramekins and place in a roasting tin. Pour enough hot water into the tin to come halfway up the sides of the ramekins. Cook for 1 1/2 hours, or until set in the centre. Cool and refrigerate until ready to serve. Just before serving, sprinkle the tops with demerara sugar and caramelize under a very hot grill (broiler) or with a blowtorch. Serve immediately.

ÎLE FLOTTANTE

THIS ROUND ISLAND OF MERINGUE FLOATING ON A SEA OF CUSTARD IS OFTEN CONFUSED WITH ANOTHER FRENCH MERINGUE DESSERT, *OEUFS A LA NEIGE*. 'FLOATING ISLAND' IS ONE LARGE BAKED MERINGUE, WHILE 'EGGS IN THE SNOW' ARE SMALL POACHED MERINGUES ON CUSTARD.

MERINGUE
4 egg whites
125 g (¹/₂ cup) caster (superfine)
   sugar
¹/₄ teaspoon vanilla extract

PRALINE
55 g (¹/₄ cup) sugar
55 g (2 oz) flaked almonds

2 quantities crème anglaise
   (page 285)

SERVES 6

PREHEAT the oven to 140°C (275°F/Gas 1) and put a roasting tin in the oven to heat up. Grease and line the base of a 1.5 litre (6 cup) charlotte mould with a circle of greaseproof paper and lightly grease the base and side.

TO MAKE the meringue, beat the egg whites in a clean dry bowl until very stiff peaks form. Whisk in the sugar gradually to make a very stiff glossy meringue. Whisk in the vanilla extract.

SPOON the meringue into the mould, smooth the surface and place a greased circle of greaseproof paper on top. Put the mould into the hot roasting tin and pour boiling water into the tin until it comes halfway up the side of the charlotte mould.

BAKE for 50–60 minutes, or until a knife poked into the centre of the meringue comes out clean. Remove the circle of paper, put a plate over the meringue and turn it over. Lift off the mould and the other circle of paper and leave to cool.

TO MAKE the praline, grease a sheet of foil and lay it out flat on the work surface. Put the sugar in a small saucepan with 3 tablespoons water and heat gently until completely dissolved. Bring to the boil and cook until deep golden, then quickly tip in the flaked almonds and pour onto the oiled foil. Spread a little and leave to cool. When the praline has hardened, grind it to a fine powder in a food processor or with a mortar and pestle.

SPRINKLE the praline over the meringue and pour a sea of warmed crème anglaise around its base. Serve in wedges with the remaining crème anglaise.

Grease and line the charlotte mould and place greased paper over the top after filling so that the meringue will not stick.

CRÊPES SUZETTE

THE ORIGIN OF THE NAME CRÊPES SUZETTE HAS BECOME A MYSTERY, BUT THEY SEEM TO HAVE APPEARED SOMETIME AT THE END OF THE NINETEENTH CENTURY. TRADITIONALLY FLAMBÉED AT THE TABLE IN RESTAURANTS, IN THIS RECIPE THE CRÊPES ARE QUICKLY SET ALIGHT ON THE STOVETOP.

CRÊPES
2 tablespoons grated orange zest
1 tablespoon grated lemon zest
1 quantity crêpe batter (page 282)

115 g (½ cup) caster (superfine) sugar
250 ml (1 cup) orange juice
1 tablespoon grated orange zest
2 tablespoons brandy or Cognac
2 tablespoons Grand Marnier
55 g (2 oz) unsalted butter, diced

SERVES 6

TO MAKE the crêpes, stir the orange and lemon zest into the crêpe batter. Heat and grease a crêpe pan. Pour in enough batter to coat the base of the pan in a thin even layer and tip out any excess. Cook over moderate heat for about a minute, or until the crêpe starts to come away from the side of the pan. Turn the crêpe and cook on the other side for 1 minute or until lightly golden. Repeat with the remaining batter. Fold the crêpes into quarters.

MELT the sugar in a large frying pan over low heat and cook to a rich caramel, tilting the pan so the caramel browns evenly. Pour in the orange juice and zest and boil for 2 minutes. Put the crêpes in the pan and spoon the sauce over them.

ADD the brandy and Grand Marnier and flambé by lighting the pan with your gas flame or a match (stand well back when you do this and keep a pan lid handy for emergencies). Add the butter and shake the pan until it melts. Serve immediately.

Once the crêpe starts to come away from the side of the pan, it is cooked enough to turn over.

CRÊPES SOUFFLÉS

CRÊPES SOUFFLÉS

1 quantity crème pâtissière (page 285)
125 ml (½ cup) orange juice
grated zest of 1 orange
2 tablespoons Grand Marnier
8 egg whites
2 tablespoons caster (superfine) sugar
½ quantity cooked crêpes (page 282)
icing (confectioners') sugar

SERVES 6

PREHEAT the oven to 200°C (400°F/Gas 6). Warm the crème pâtissière in a bowl over a saucepan of simmering water and whisk in the orange juice, orange zest and Grand Marnier.

BEAT the egg whites in a clean dry bowl until firm peaks form. Whisk in the sugar gradually to make a stiff glossy meringue. Whisk half into the crème pâtissière to loosen the mixture, then fold in the rest with a large metal spoon or spatula. Place two big spoonfuls of soufflé on the centre of each crêpe. Fold in half with a spatula, without pressing. Bake on a buttered baking tray for 5 minutes. Dust with icing sugar and serve immediately.

Saint Cyprien in the Dordogne.

CARAMEL ICE CREAM

ALTHOUGH WE ALL THINK OF ICE CREAM AS A FROZEN DESSERT, IT SHOULD IDEALLY BE SERVED WHEN IT IS JUST ON THE VERGE OF MELTING. IF YOU SERVE IT TOO COLD THE FLAVOUR WILL BE MASKED, SO TAKE IT OUT OF THE FREEZER HALF AN HOUR BEFORE SERVING TO LET IT SOFTEN.

60 g ($^1/_4$ cup) sugar
80 ml ($^1/_3$ cup) cream
3 egg yolks
330 ml (1$^1/_3$ cups) milk
1 vanilla pod

SERVES 4

TO MAKE the caramel, put 45 g of the sugar in a heavy-based saucepan and heat until it dissolves and starts to caramelize—tip the saucepan from side to side as the sugar cooks to keep the colouring even. Remove from the heat and carefully add the cream (it will splutter). Stir over low heat until the caramel remelts.

WHISK the egg yolks and remaining sugar until light and fluffy. Put the milk and vanilla pod in a saucepan and bring just to the boil, then strain over the caramel. Bring back to the boil and pour over the egg yolk mixture, whisking continuously.

POUR the custard back into the saucepan and cook, stirring, until it is thick enough to coat the back of a wooden spoon. Do not let it boil or the custard will split. Pass through a sieve into a bowl and leave over ice to cool quickly.

CHURN in an ice-cream maker following the manufacturer's instructions. Alternatively, pour into a plastic freezer box, cover and freeze. Stir every 30 minutes with a whisk during freezing to break up the ice crystals and give a better texture. Freeze overnight with a layer of plastic wrap over the surface and the lid on the container. Keep in the freezer until ready to serve.

Add the hot milk to the caramel, then pour over the egg yolk mixture to make a custard.

BLACKCURRANT SORBET

WE'VE USED GLUCOSE FOR THIS SORBET BECAUSE IT STOPS THE SUGAR CRYSTALLIZING AND GIVES A GOOD TEXTURE. TO WEIGH GLUCOSE WITHOUT IT RUNNING EVERYWHERE, MEASURE THE SUGAR INTO THE PAN OF THE SCALES, THEN MAKE A HOLLOW IN THE MIDDLE AND POUR IN THE GLUCOSE.

230 g (1 cup) caster (superfine) sugar
30 g (1 oz) liquid glucose
350 g (12 oz) blackcurrants, stalks removed
1 tablespoon lemon juice
2 tablespoons crème de cassis

SERVES 4

PUT the sugar and glucose in a saucepan with 225 ml (8 fl oz) water. Heat gently to dissolve the sugar, then boil for 2–3 minutes. Cool completely.

PUT the blackcurrants and lemon juice in a blender with half of the cooled syrup and mix to a thick purée. (Alternatively, push the fruit through a sieve to purée and then mix with the lemon juice and syrup.) Add the remaining syrup and the crème de cassis and mix well.

CHURN in an ice-cream maker following the manufacturer's instructions. Alternatively, pour into a plastic freezer box, cover and freeze. Stir every 30 minutes with a whisk during freezing to break up the ice crystals and give a better texture. Freeze overnight with a layer of plastic wrap over the surface and the lid on the container. Keep in the freezer until ready to serve.

RED WINE SORBET

250 g (9 oz) caster (superfine) sugar
100 ml (3 1/2 fl oz) orange juice
250 ml (1 cup) light red wine

SERVES 4

DISSOLVE the caster sugar in 250 ml (1 cup) boiling water, stirring until it has completely dissolved. Add the orange juice and red wine and stir well.

CHURN in an ice-cream maker following the manufacturer's instructions. Alternatively, pour into a plastic freezer box, cover and freeze. Stir every 30 minutes with a whisk during freezing to break up the ice crystals and give a better texture. Freeze overnight with a layer of plastic wrap over the surface and the lid on the container. Keep in the freezer until ready to serve.

Stir the sugar until it is completely dissolved before adding the orange juice and wine.

PÂTISSERIE is one of France's most respected culinary arts, one that is even protected by its own patron saint, Saint Honoré. Pâtissiers can become members of several professional organizations, such as The National Confederation of Pastry Chefs and Relais Desserts International Professional Organization of Master Pastry Makers. One of these signs hanging above a pâtisserie shows a real commitment to the trade.

PÂTISSERIE

PÂTISSERIE, THE ART OF CAKE AND PASTRY MAKING, IS THE MOST DELIGHTFUL AND ELABORATE OF CULINARY ARTS—THE ONLY ONE WHERE BEAUTIFUL DECORATION CARRIES EQUAL WEIGHT TO THE FLAVOUR OF THE FOOD.

Pâtisserie can be traced back to the simple cakes of the ancient world and the pastry-making of the Middle-East, with its use of spices, nuts and sugar. From the Crusades onwards, these techniques and ingredients filtered into Europe, particularly Italy, and when in the sixteenth century Catherine de Medici arrived at the French court with her retinue of Italian chefs, they revolutionized French pâtisserie with their skills, such as the invention of choux pastry. In the early nineteenth century, Antonin Carême became the first of a line of great Parisian pâtissiers (pastry chefs). He was famous for his fantastical architectural creations, including croquembouches shaped into famous buildings.

BUYING PÂTISSERIE

Pâtisserie refers not only to the pastries, but also to the place where they are made and sold. Pâtisseries are sometimes solely shops, but often have a salon de thé attached where patrons can enjoy a pâtisserie in the mid-morning or afternoon, the favoured times for indulging in such a treat. Pâtisseries also sell candied fruits, chocolates, beautiful items to finish a meal or present as a gift. They display their pâtisserie elegantly, and after carefully choosing, customers are presented with their purchases beautifully wrapped.

JOËL DURAND'S chocolates in his Saint Rémy shop are each numbered and described on a 'menu'. He flavours chocolate with Provençal lavender and herbs, green tea, sichuan pepper and jasmine. The flavours change with the season—number 28 is perfumed with rose petals in summer and Carmargue saffron the rest of the year. Number 30, known as 'Provence', is a mix of olives from Les Baux and praline.

REGIONAL PÂTISSERIE

Each area of France has its own pâtisserie specialities. In Alsace-Lorraine in the Northeast, there are Austrian-inspired Kugelhopf and strudels and wonderful fruit tarts, especially those using mirabelle plums. Paris is famed for its pâtisserie shops and dark, bitter chocolate is a northern speciality, especially in the cork-shaped *bouchons* from Champagne. In the Northwest, Brittany and Normandy's dairy farming and apples are used to create buttery Breton biscuits and the finest tarte aux pommes. In the East and Centre, Lyon is home to Bernachon, one of France's finest *pâtisseries-confiseries*, while pain d'épices, a spicy gingerbread, has been made in Dijon since the fifteenth century. The Southwest is known for its rural Basque cooking, which includes gâteau basque, as well as famous macarons from Saint Emilion and tarts made with Agen prunes. In the South, with its abundance of fruit, there are candied fruit and marrons (chestnuts).

FRUIT CONFITS are a speciality of Provence, and were originally a way to store soft fruit through the winter. Lilamand Confiseur is one of the last independent producers of the jewel-like fruits, which must be made with fruits flavourful enough to be tasted through the sugar.

PITHIVIERS

ORIGINATING IN PITHIVIERS IN THE LOIRE VALLEY, THIS PASTRY IS TRADITIONALLY SERVED ON TWELFTH NIGHT, WHEN IT IS KNOWN AS *GALETTE DES ROIS* AND USUALLY CONTAINS A BEAN THAT BRINGS GOOD LUCK TO WHOEVER FINDS IT IN THEIR SLICE.

FILLING
140 g (5 oz) unsalted butter, at
 room temperature
145 g (²/₃ cup) caster (superfine)
 sugar
2 large eggs, lightly beaten
2 tablespoons dark rum
finely grated zest of 1 small orange
 or lemon
140 g (1¹/₃ cups) ground almonds
1 tablespoon plain (all-purpose) flour

1 quantity puff pastry (page 281)
1 egg, lightly beaten
icing (confectioners') sugar

SERVES 6

TO MAKE the filling, beat the butter and sugar together until pale and creamy. Mix in the beaten eggs, little by little, beating well after each addition. Beat in the rum and the orange or lemon zest and then lightly fold in the almonds and flour. Put the filling in the fridge to firm a little while you roll out the pastry.

CUT the pastry in half and roll out one half. Cut out a 28 cm (11 inch) circle and place the circle on a large baking tray lined with baking paper. Spread the filling over the pastry, leaving a clear border of about 2 cm (³/₄ inch) all the way round. Brush a little beaten egg over the clear border to help the two halves stick together.

ROLL OUT the other half of the pastry and cut out a second circle the same size as the first. Lay this circle on top of the filling and firmly press the edges of the pastry together. Cover and leave in the fridge for at least 1 hour (several hours or even overnight is fine).

PREHEAT the oven to 220°C (425°F/Gas 7). Brush all over the top of the pie with the beaten egg to give it a shiny glaze—be careful not to brush egg on the side of the pie or the layers won't rise properly. Working from the centre to the outside edge, score the top of the pithiviers with curved lines in a spiral pattern.

BAKE the pithiviers for 25–30 minutes, or until it is well risen and golden brown. Dust with icing sugar and allow to cool. Cut into slices to serve.

Leave a clear border around the filling, then brush it with egg to help the two halves of the pastry stick together.

PARIS-BREST

THIS LARGE CHOUX PASTRY CAKE WAS NAMED AFTER THE PARIS-BREST BICYCLE RACE. IT WAS INVENTED IN 1891 BY A CANNY PARISIAN PASTRY CHEF WHO OWNED A SHOP ALONG THE ROUTE AND HAD THE IDEA OF PRODUCING THESE BICYCLE WHEEL-SHAPED CAKES.

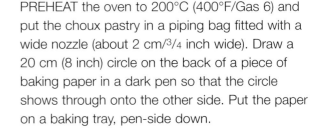

1 quantity choux pastry (page 282)
1 egg, lightly beaten
1 tablespoon flaked almonds
1 quantity crème pâtissière
  (page 285)
icing (confectioners') sugar

PRALINE
115 g (1/2 cup) caster (superfine)
  sugar
90 g (1 cup) flaked almonds

SERVES 6

PREHEAT the oven to 200°C (400°F/Gas 6) and put the choux pastry in a piping bag fitted with a wide nozzle (about 2 cm/3/4 inch wide). Draw a 20 cm (8 inch) circle on the back of a piece of baking paper in a dark pen so that the circle shows through onto the other side. Put the paper on a baking tray, pen-side down.

PIPE a ring of pastry over the guide you have drawn. Now pipe another ring of pastry directly inside this one so that you have one thick ring. Pipe another two circles on top of the first two and continue until all the choux pastry has been used. Brush the choux ring with beaten egg and sprinkle with the flaked almonds.

BAKE the choux ring for 20–30 minutes, then reduce the oven to 180°C (350°F/Gas 4) and bake for a further 20–25 minutes. Remove from the baking tray and place on a wire rack. Immediately slice the ring in half horizontally, making the base twice as deep as the top. Lift off the top and scoop out any uncooked pastry from the base. Leave to cool completely.

TO MAKE the praline, grease a sheet of foil and lay it out flat on the work surface. Put the sugar in a small saucepan with 125 ml (1/2 cup) water and heat gently until completely dissolved. Bring to the boil and cook until deep golden, then quickly tip in the flaked almonds and pour onto the oiled foil. Spread a little and leave to cool. When the praline has hardened, grind it to a fine powder in a food processor or with a mortar and pestle. Mix into the cold crème pâtissière.

SPOON the crème pâtissière into the base of the choux pastry ring and cover with the top. Dust with icing sugar to serve.

Pipe a double thickness ring of choux pastry over the guide.

APPLE TART

1 quantity sweet pastry (page 278)
1/2 quantity crème pâtissière
    (page 285)
4 dessert apples
80 g (1/4 cup) apricot jam (jelly)

SERVES 8

PREHEAT the oven to 180°C (350°F/Gas 4). Roll out the pastry to line a 23 cm (9 inch) round loose-based fluted tart tin. Chill for 20 minutes.

LINE the pastry shell with a crumpled piece of greaseproof paper and baking beads (use dried beans or rice if you don't have beads). Blind bake the pastry for 10 minutes, remove the paper and beads and bake for a further 3–5 minutes, or until the pastry is just cooked but still very pale.

FILL the pastry with the crème pâtissière. Peel and core the apples, cut them in half and then into thin slices. Arrange over the top of the tart and bake for 25–30 minutes or until the apples are golden and the pastry is cooked. Leave to cool completely, then melt the apricot jam with 1 tablespoon water, sieve out any lumps and brush over the apples to make them shine.

APPLE TART

TARTE AU CITRON

1 quantity sweet pastry (page 278)

FILLING
4 eggs
2 egg yolks
285 g (1 1/4 cups) caster (superfine)
    sugar
185 ml (3/4 cup) thick
    (double/heavy) cream
250 ml (1 cup) lemon juice
finely grated zest of 3 lemons

SERVES 8

PREHEAT the oven to 190°C (375°F/Gas 5). Roll out the pastry to line a 23 cm (9 inch) round loose-based fluted tart tin. Chill for 20 minutes.

TO MAKE the filling, whisk together the eggs, egg yolks and sugar. Add the cream, whisking all the time, and then the lemon juice and zest.

LINE the pastry shell with a crumpled piece of greaseproof paper and baking beads (use dried beans or rice if you don't have beads). Blind bake the pastry for 10 minutes, remove the paper and beads and bake for a further 3–5 minutes, or until the pastry is just cooked but still very pale. Remove from the oven and reduce the temperature to 150°C (300°F/Gas 2).

PUT the tin on a baking tray and carefully pour the filling into the pastry case. Return to the oven for 35–40 minutes, or until the filling has set. Leave to cool completely before serving.

Whisking the lemon filling for the tarte au citron.

MIXED BERRY TARTLETS

1 quantity sweet pastry (page 278)
1 quantity frangipane (page 285)
400 g (14 oz) mixed berries
3 tablespoons apricot jam (jelly)

MAKES 10

PREHEAT the oven to 180°C (350°F/Gas 4).
Roll out the pastry to a thickness of 2 mm (1/8 inch)
and use to line ten 8 cm- (3 inch-) wide tartlet
tins. Put the frangipane in a piping bag and pipe
into the tartlet tins. Put the tins on a baking tray
and bake for 10–12 minutes, or until golden.

COOL SLIGHTLY on a wire rack, then arrange the
berries on top. Melt the jam with 1 teaspoon
water, sieve out any lumps and brush over the
berries to make them shine.

MIXED BERRY TARTLETS

PEAR AND ALMOND TART

1 quantity sweet pastry (page 278)
55 g (1/4 cup) caster (superfine)
   sugar
1 vanilla pod
3 pears (ripe but still firm), peeled,
   halved and cored
3 tablespoons apricot jam (jelly)

ALMOND FILLING
150 g (51/2 oz) unsalted butter,
   softened
145 g (2/3 cup) caster (superfine)
   sugar
few drops of vanilla extract
2 large eggs, lightly beaten
140 g (11/3 cups) ground almonds
finely grated zest of 1 small lemon
30 g (1/4 cup) plain (all-purpose)
   flour

SERVES 8

PREHEAT the oven to 190°C (375°F/Gas 5). Roll
out the pastry to line a 23 cm (9 inch) round
loose-based fluted tart tin. Chill for 20 minutes.

PUT the sugar and vanilla pod in a saucepan. Add
the pears and pour in just enough water to cover
them, then remove the pears. Bring the water to a
simmer and cook for 5 minutes. Add the pears,
cover and poach for 5–10 minutes until tender.
Drain and leave to cool.

TO MAKE the almond filling, beat the butter, sugar
and vanilla extract together until pale and creamy.
Beat in the eggs gradually and then fold in the
almonds, lemon zest and flour.

LINE the pastry shell with a crumpled piece of
greaseproof paper and baking beads (use dried
beans or rice if you don't have beads). Blind bake
the pastry for 10 minutes, remove the paper and
beads and bake for a further 3–5 minutes, or until
the pastry is just cooked but still very pale. Reduce
the oven temperature to 180°C (350°F/Gas 4).

SPREAD three-quarters of the filling in the pastry
shell and put the pear halves on top, cut side
down and stalk ends in the middle. Fill the gaps
with the remaining filling. Bake for 35–40 minutes,
or until the filling is golden and firm. Melt the jam
with 1 teaspoon water, sieve out any lumps and
brush over the pears to make them shine.

Arrange the pears cut side down
in the pastry shell with the stalks
pointing to the centre.

APPLES AND PEARS IN PASTRY

IN LATE SUMMER AND AUTUMN, WHEN THE ORCHARDS ARE OVERFLOWING WITH FRUIT, THE NORMAN COOK MAKES *BOURDELOTS* OR *DOUILLONS*. THESE PASTRY-WRAPPED APPLES OR PEARS COULD ALSO CONTAIN A DRIZZLE OF CALVADOS.

PASTRY
150 g (5^1/$_2$ oz) unsalted butter
220 g (1^3/$_4$ cups) plain (all-purpose)
    flour
30 g (1 oz) caster (superfine) sugar
1 egg yolk

HAZELNUT FILLING
30 g (1 oz) hazelnuts, finely
    chopped
60 g (2^1/$_4$ oz) unsalted butter,
    softened
80 g (^{1}/$_3$ cup) soft brown sugar
pinch of mixed spice

2 dessert apples
2 pears (ripe but still firm)
juice of 1 lemon
1 egg, lightly beaten

SERVES 4

TO MAKE the pastry, rub the butter into the flour until the mixture resembles fine breadcrumbs. Stir in the sugar. Add the egg yolk and 40–50 ml (2–2^1/$_2$ tablespoons) water and stir with a knife to form a dough. Turn out and bring together with your hands. Wrap in plastic wrap and refrigerate for at least 30 minutes. Preheat the oven to 200°C (400°F/Gas 6) and preheat the grill (broiler).

TO MAKE the hazelnut filling, toast the hazelnuts under the hot grill (broiler) for 1–2 minutes or until browned, then cool. Mix the softened butter with the sugar, hazelnuts and mixed spice. Peel and core the apples and pears, leaving the stalks and trimming the bases of the pears if they are very big. Roll in the lemon juice and stuff with the hazelnut filling.

ROLL OUT the pastry to make a 32 cm (13 inch) square, trimming off any untidy edges. Cut into four equal squares and place an apple or pear in the centre of each. Brush the edges of the pastry with water and then bring them up so that the corners of each pastry square meet at the top of the fruit. Press the edges together so that the pastry follows the curve of the fruit.

Bring up the corners of the pastry square so they meet at the top of the fruit.

CUT OFF the excess pastry and crimp the edges to seal the fruit parcels thoroughly. Use the pastry trimmings to cut out leaves, then stick these onto the fruit by brushing the backs with water.

BRUSH the pastry fruits with the beaten egg to glaze and bake on a lightly greased baking tray for 35–40 minutes or until the pastry is cooked and browned. Serve with cream.

Dinner in Saint Rémy.

TARTE TATIN

THIS FAMOUS DESSERT IS NAMED AFTER THE TATIN SISTERS WHO RAN A RESTAURANT NEAR ORLÉANS AT THE BEGINNING OF THE TWENTIETH CENTURY. THEY CERTAINLY POPULARIZED THE DISH, BUT MAY NOT HAVE INVENTED IT THEMSELVES.

1.5 kg (3 lb 5 oz) dessert apples
70 g (2¹/₂ oz) unsalted butter
170 g (³/₄ cup) caster (superfine) sugar
1 quantity tart pastry (page 278)

CRÈME CHANTILLY
185 ml (³/₄ cup) thick (double/heavy) cream
1 teaspoon icing (confectioners') sugar
¹/₂ teaspon vanilla extract

SERVES 8

PEEL, CORE and cut the apples into quarters. Put the butter and sugar in a deep 25 cm (10 inch) frying pan with an ovenproof handle. Heat until the butter and sugar have melted together. Arrange the apples tightly, one by one, in the frying pan, making sure there are no gaps. Remember that you will be turning the tart out the other way up, so arrange the apple pieces so that they are neat underneath.

COOK over low heat for 35–40 minutes, or until the apple is soft, the caramel lightly browned and any excess liquid has evaporated. Baste the apple with a pastry brush every so often, so that the top is caramelized as well. Preheat the oven to 190°C (375°F/Gas 5).

ROLL OUT the pastry on a lightly floured surface into a circle slightly larger than the frying pan and about 3 mm (¹/₈ inch) thick. Lay the pastry over the apple and press down around the edge to enclose it completely. Roughly trim the edge of the pastry and then fold the edge back on itself to give a neat finish.

BAKE FOR 25–30 minutes, or until the pastry is golden and cooked. Remove from the oven and leave to rest for 5 minutes before turning out. (If any apple sticks to the pan, just push it back into the hole in the tart.)

TO MAKE the crème chantilly, put the cream, icing sugar and vanilla extract in a chilled bowl. Whisk until soft peaks form and then serve with the hot tarte tatin.

Wedge the apples tightly into the pan—they shrink as they cook.

STRAWBERRY MILLEFEUILLE

1 quantity puff pastry (page 281)
5 tablespoons sugar
¹/₂ quantity crème pâtissière
  (page 285)
125 ml (¹/₂ cup) whipping cream
300 g (10¹/₂ oz) strawberries, cut
  into quarters
icing (confectioners') sugar

SERVES 6

PREHEAT the oven to 180°C (350°F/Gas 4). Roll out the puff pastry on a lightly floured surface into a rectangle about 2 mm (¹/₈ inch) thick. Roll the pastry around a rolling pin, then unroll it onto a baking tray lined with baking paper. Leave in the fridge for 15 minutes.

TO MAKE the syrup, put the sugar and 185 ml (³/₄ cup) water in a saucepan. Boil for 5 minutes, then remove from the heat.

CUT OUT three 30 x 13 cm (12 x 5 inch) rectangles from the pastry and place them on a large baking tray. Prick with a fork, cover with a sheet of baking paper and place a second baking tray on top to prevent the pastry rising unevenly. Bake for 6 minutes, then remove the top baking tray and baking paper. Brush the pastry with the syrup and bake for another 6 minutes or until golden on top. Cool on a wire rack.

WHISK the crème pâtissière. Whip the cream and fold into the crème pâtissière. Spread half of this over one pastry rectangle and top with half of the strawberries. Place a second layer of pastry on top and spread with the remaining cream and strawberries. Cover with the last layer of pastry and dust with icing sugar to serve.

Madeleines are baked in small scallop-shaped moulds.

MADELEINES

3 eggs
115 g (¹/₂ cup) caster (superfine)
  sugar
155 g (1¹/₄ cups) plain (all-purpose)
  flour
100 g (3¹/₂ oz) unsalted butter,
  melted
grated zest of 1 lemon and
  1 orange

MAKES 14 (OR 30 SMALL ONES)

PREHEAT the oven to 200°C (400°F/Gas 6). Brush a tray of madeleine moulds with melted butter and coat with flour, then tap the tray to remove the excess flour.

WHISK the eggs and sugar until the mixture is thick and pale and the whisk leaves a trail when lifted. Gently fold in the flour, then the melted butter and grated lemon and orange zest. Spoon into the moulds, leaving a little room for rising. Bake for 12 minutes (small madeleines will only need 7 minutes), or until very lightly golden and springy to the touch. Remove from the tray and cool on a wire rack.

MADELEINES

GÂTEAU BASQUE

THE BASQUE COUNTRY IS SQUEEZED INTO THE SOUTHWESTERN CORNER OF FRANCE, BORDERED BY THE SEA ON ONE SIDE AND SPAIN ON THE OTHER. JUST ABOUT EVERY BASQUE HOUSEHOLD HAS ITS OWN RECIPE FOR THIS BAKED TART, WHICH IS ALSO KNOWN AS *VÉRITABLE PASTIZA*.

Use the best-quality thick jam (jelly) you can find to spread over the pastry shell. Spoon in the crème pâtissière over the top.

ALMOND PASTRY
400 g (3¼ cups) plain (all-purpose) flour
1 teaspoon finely grated lemon zest
55 g (½ cup) ground almonds
145 g (⅔ cup) caster (superfine) sugar
1 egg
1 egg yolk
¼ teaspoon vanilla extract
150 g (5½ oz) unsalted butter, softened

ALMOND CRÈME PÂTISSIÈRE
6 egg yolks
200 g (7 oz) caster (superfine) sugar
60 g (½ cup) plain (all-purpose) flour
55 g (½ cup) ground almonds
1 litre (4 cups) milk
4 vanilla pods

4 tablespoons thick black cherry or plum jam (jelly)
1 egg, lightly beaten

SERVES 8

TO MAKE the pastry, mix the flour, lemon zest and almonds together, tip onto a work surface and make a well in the centre. Put the sugar, egg, egg yolk, vanilla extract and butter in the well.

MIX TOGETHER the sugar, eggs and butter, using a pecking action with your fingertips and thumb. Once they are mixed, use the edge of a palette knife to incorporate the flour, flicking it onto the dough and then chopping through it. Bring the dough together with your hands. Wrap in plastic wrap and put in the fridge for at least 30 minutes.

ROLL OUT two-thirds of the pastry to fit a 25 cm (10 inch) tart ring. Trim the edge and chill in the fridge for another 30 minutes. Preheat the oven to 180°C (350°F/Gas 4).

TO MAKE the almond crème pâtissière, whisk together the egg yolks and sugar until pale and creamy. Sift in the flour and ground almonds and mix together well. Put the milk in a saucepan. Split the vanilla pods in two, scrape out the seeds and add the whole lot to the milk. Bring just to the boil and then strain over the egg yolk mixture, stirring continuously. Pour back into the clean saucepan and bring to the boil, stirring constantly—it will be lumpy at first but will become smooth as you stir. Boil for 2 minutes, then leave to cool.

SPREAD the jam over the base of the pastry case, then spread with the crème pâtissière. Roll out the remaining pastry to make a top for the pie. Brush the edge of the pastry case with beaten egg, put the pastry top over it and press together around the side. Trim the edge. Brush the top of the pie with beaten egg and gently score in a crisscross pattern. Bake for 40 minutes, or until golden brown. Cool for at least 30 minutes before serving, either slightly warm or cold.

RAISIN RUM BABA

THE BABA IS THOUGHT TO HAVE ITS ORIGINS IN POLAND AND WAS INTRODUCED TO FRANCE BY A PARISIAN PASTRY COOK AFTER A VISIT BY THE POLISH COURT. BABAS CAN BE MADE IN DARIOLE MOULDS OR IN SAVARIN TINS, AS HERE.

3 teaspoons dried yeast or 20 g
  (3/4 oz) fresh yeast
80 ml (1/3 cup) warm milk
1 tablespoon caster (superfine)
  sugar
1 large egg
2 large egg yolks
finely grated zest of 1 small orange
165 g (1 1/3 cups) plain (all-purpose)
  flour
50 g (1/2 cup) raisins
50 g (1 3/4 oz) unsalted butter,
  melted

ORANGE RUM SYRUP
230 g (1 cup) caster (superfine)
  sugar
2 tablespoons orange juice
4 tablespoons dark rum

SERVES 8

MIX the yeast with half of the warm milk and 1 teaspoon of the sugar. Leave for 10 minutes in a warm place until the yeast becomes frothy. If the yeast does not bubble and foam in this time, throw it away and start again.

WHISK together the egg, egg yolks and remaining sugar and stir in the orange zest. Sift the flour into a large bowl and make a well in the centre. Pour the yeast mixture and egg mixture into the well and add the raisins. Gradually stir in the flour, dribbling in the rest of the warm milk as you do so. Once the ingredients are thoroughly mixed, add the melted butter, little by little, mixing well. Work the dough with your hands for 10 minutes, lifting it high and dropping it into the bowl, until the dough is very soft. Cover with oiled plastic wrap and leave to rise in a warm place for 1 1/4 hours or until the dough has doubled in size.

TO MAKE the orange rum syrup, put the sugar in a saucepan with 350 ml (12 fl oz) water. Bring to the boil, and boil for 3 minutes. Remove from the heat and add the orange juice and rum. Set aside.

KNOCK BACK the dough by punching it with your fist several times to expel the air, and then lightly knead it again for a minute. Put it in a buttered 1.25 litre (5 cup) savarin tin. Cover with oiled plastic wrap and leave to rise in a warm place for 20–30 minutes, or until risen almost to the top of the tin. Preheat the oven to 190°C (375°F/Gas 5).

BAKE the baba for 25–30 minutes, covering the top with foil if it is overbrowning. Remove from the oven and, while still in the tin, prick all over the top of the baba with a skewer. Drizzle some of the syrup over the top of the baba and leave to soak in before drizzling with the rest. Leave for 15 minutes, before turning out onto a large serving plate to serve.

Bake the rum baba in the buttered savarin tin. Leave it in the tin while you drizzle the syrup over the top, letting the syrup soak in completely.

BASICS

BRIOCHE

BRIOCHE IS SO BUTTERY THAT YOU CAN SERVE IT UP FOR BREAKFAST WITH NOTHING MORE FANCY THAN A LITTLE GOOD-QUALITY JAM (JELLY) OR CURD. IF YOU HAVE ONE, USE A FLUTED BRIOCHE TIN, IF NOT, AN ORDINARY LOAF TIN WILL BE FINE.

Because brioche dough has so much butter in it, you will notice that it is heavier to knead than bread dough.

2 teaspoons dried yeast or 15 g
  ($1/2$ oz) fresh yeast
60 ml ($1/4$ cup) warm milk
2 tablespoons caster (superfine)
  sugar
220 g ($1^3/4$ cups) plain (all-purpose)
  flour
pinch of salt
2 large eggs, lightly beaten
few drops vanilla extract
75 g ($2^1/2$ oz) butter, cubed
lightly beaten egg, to glaze

MAKES 1 LOAF

MIX the yeast with the warm milk and 1 teaspoon of the sugar. Leave for 10 minutes in a warm place until the yeast becomes frothy. If the yeast docs not bubble and foam in this time, throw it away and start again.

SIFT the flour into a large bowl and sprinkle with the salt and the rest of the sugar. Make a well in the centre and add the eggs, vanilla extract and yeast mixture. Use a wooden spoon to mix all the ingredients together, then use your hands to knead the dough for a minute to bring it together. Transfer to a lightly floured work surface and gradually knead in the butter, piece by piece. Knead for 5 minutes, then put the dough into a clean bowl and cover with oiled plastic wrap. Leave to rise in a draught-free spot for 1–1$1/2$ hours or until the dough has doubled in size.

KNOCK BACK the dough by punching it with your fist several times to expel the air, and then lightly knead it again for a couple of minutes. Shape the dough into a rectangle and place in a 20 x 7 x 9 cm (8 x 2$3/4$ x 3$1/2$ inch) buttered loaf tin. Cover with oiled plastic wrap and leave to rise in a draught-free spot for 30–35 minutes, or until risen almost to the top of the tin. Preheat the oven to 200°C (400°F/Gas 6).

ONCE the brioche has risen, use a pair of scissors to carefully snip into the top of the dough at regular intervals. Snip three times on each side and twice at each end. The cuts should only be about 2.5 cm (1 inch) deep. Brush the top with egg to glaze and bake for 30–35 minutes, or until the top of the brioche is rich brown. Turn the hot brioche out of the tin and tap the bottom of the loaf—if it sounds hollow, it is cooked. Put the brioche back in the tin upside down and return to the oven for 5 minutes to crisp the base of the loaf. Transfer to a wire rack and leave to cool.

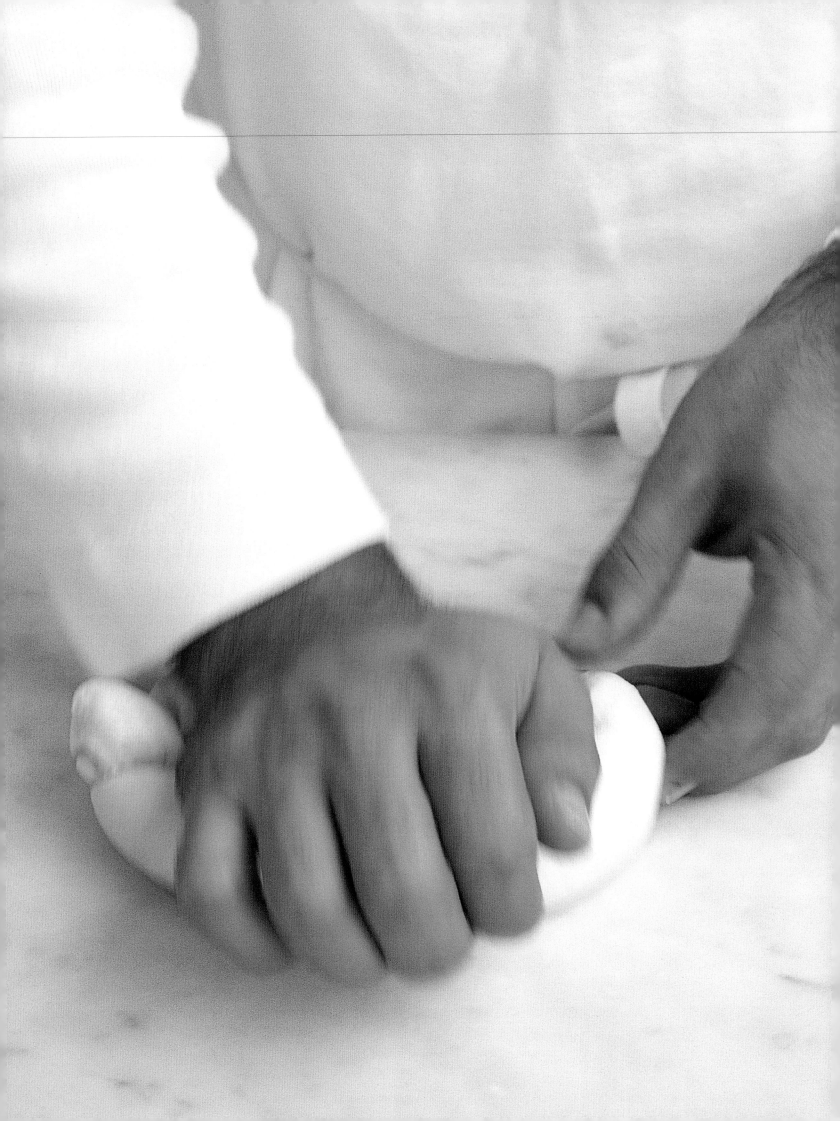

BREAD DOUGH

LUNCH ON THICK SLICES OF THIS RUSTIC BREAD WITH UNSALTED BUTTER AND A GOOD CHEESE. THIS IS A BASIC BREAD DOUGH AND IS EASILY FLAVOURED—YOU COULD ADD CHOPPED WALNUTS, FRESH HERBS, OLIVES OR CHEESE.

2 teaspoons dried yeast or 15 g
   (1/2 oz) fresh yeast
250 g (2 cups) strong plain
   (all-purpose) flour
1/2 teaspoon salt
3 tablespoons olive oil

MAKES 1 LOAF

MIX the yeast with 125 ml (1/2 cup) warm water. Leave for 10 minutes in a warm place until the yeast becomes frothy. If the yeast does not bubble and foam in this time, throw it away and start again.

SIFT the flour into a large bowl and add the salt, olive oil and the yeast mixture. Mix until the dough clumps together and forms a ball.

TURN OUT onto a lightly floured work surface. Knead the dough, adding a little more flour or a few drops of warm water if necessary, until you have a soft dough that is not sticky but is dry to the touch. Knead for 10 minutes, or until smooth, and the impression made by a finger springs back immediately.

RUB the inside of a large bowl with olive oil. Roll the ball of dough around in the bowl to coat it with oil, then cut a shallow cross on the top of the ball with a sharp knife. Leave the dough in the bowl, cover with a tea towel or put in a plastic bag and leave in a draught-free spot for 1–1 1/2 hours or until the dough has doubled in size (or leave in the fridge for 8 hours to rise slowly).

KNOCK BACK the dough by punching it with your fist several times to expel the air and then knead it again for a couple of minutes. (At this stage the dough can be stored in the fridge for 4 hours, or frozen. Bring back to room temperature before continuing.) Leave in a warm place to rise until doubled in size. Place in a tin, on a baking tray or use as directed in the recipe, then bake at 230°C (450°F/Gas 8) for 30 minutes. When cooked, the base of the bread will sound hollow when tapped.

Use flour that is packaged as 'strong' or 'bread' flour. You can use plain (all-purpose) flour or a mixture of plain and wholemeal, but the results won't be as good.

TART PASTRY

220 g (1³/4 cups) plain (all-purpose)
  flour
pinch of salt
150 g (5¹/2 oz) unsalted butter,
  chilled and diced
1 egg yolk

MAKES 450 G (1 LB)

SIFT the flour and salt into a large bowl, add the butter and rub in with your fingertips until the mixture resembles breadcrumbs. Add the egg yolk and a little cold water (about 2–3 teaspoons) and mix with the blade of a palette knife until the dough just starts to come together. Bring the dough together with your hands and shape into a ball. Wrap in plastic wrap and put in the fridge to rest for at least 30 minutes. (You can make the dough in a food processor, using the pulse button.)

ROLL OUT the pastry into a circle on a lightly floured surface and use to line a tart tin, as directed in the recipe. Trim the edge and pinch up the pastry edge to make an even border raised slightly above the rim of the tin. Slide onto a baking tray and rest in the fridge for 10 minutes.

When making the sweet pastry it is easiest to work directly on the work surface.

SWEET PASTRY

340 g (2³/4 cups) plain (all-purpose)
  flour
small pinch of salt
150 g (5¹/2 oz) unsalted butter
90 g (³/4 cup) icing (confectioners')
  sugar
2 eggs, beaten

MAKES 700 G (1 LB 9 OZ)

SIFT the flour and salt onto a work surface and make a well in the centre. Put the butter into the well and work, using a pecking action with your fingertips and thumb, until it is very soft. Add the sugar to the butter and mix together. Add the eggs to the butter and mix together.

GRADUALLY incorporate the flour, flicking it onto the mixture and then chopping through it until you have a rough dough. Bring together with your hands and then knead a few times to make a smooth dough. Roll into a ball, wrap in plastic wrap and put in the fridge for at least 1 hour.

ROLL OUT the pastry into a circle on a lightly floured surface and use to line a tart tin, as directed in the recipe. Trim the edge and pinch up the pastry edge to make an even border raised slightly above the rim of the tin. Slide onto a baking tray and rest in the fridge for 10 minutes.

SWEET PASTRY

PUFF PASTRY

LIGHTNESS IS THE HALLMARK OF GOOD PUFF PASTRY AND THE MANY LAYERS SHOULD RISE WITHOUT STICKING. THE KEY IS TO HAVE THE BUTTER AND PASTRY AT THE SAME CONSISTENCY WHEN YOU ROLL THEM OUT, AND TO KEEP THE ROLLING AND FOLDING AS NEAT AS YOU CAN.

250 g (2 cups) plain (all-purpose) flour
1 teaspoon lemon juice
1 teaspoon salt
25 g (1 oz) butter, melted
200 g (7 oz) butter, chilled

MAKES 650 G (1 LB 7 OZ)

SIFT the flour into a bowl and make a well in the centre. Pour in 125 ml ($^1/_2$ cup) water, the lemon juice, salt and melted butter. Draw in the flour with your fingertips, little by little, until you have a rough dough. Turn out onto a work surface and knead with the heel of your hand until the dough is smooth. Shape into a ball and cut a cross on the top. Wrap with plastic wrap and refrigerate for 1–2 hours.

PLACE the chilled butter between two pieces of greaseproof paper and beat with a rolling pin to make a square 1–2 cm ($^1/_2$–$^3/_4$ inch) thick. Keep the butter cool so that it doesn't harden again or melt further—it needs to be the same softness as the pastry or it will break up when you roll it.

ON A LIGHTLY floured surface, roll out the dough in four different directions to form a cross large enough to hold the square of butter in its centre. Put the butter in the centre and fold the four arms of dough over it, one by one, to enclose the butter completely. Position the dough so that it looks like a book with the spine to the left and the open piece of dough to the right. Roll the pastry away from you into a rectangle, keeping the corners as square as you can, then fold the top third down and the bottom third up to make a parcel of three even layers. Turn the pastry 90 degrees to the right and repeat the rolling, folding and turning, trying to keep the corners neat and square—this will help make the pastry layers even. Wrap in plastic wrap and chill for 30 minutes. (You can mark the pastry with finger indents each time you refrigerate so you remember how many turns you have made.)

REPOSITION the pastry as before, with the hinge to your left, then roll out, fold, turn and chill twice more. Rest for 30 minutes, then make two more turns as before. The pastry is now ready to use.

Although it can be time-consuming to make, home-made puff pastry that uses butter will always taste better than commercial pastry, which is often made with vegetable fat.

CHOUX PASTRY

150 g (5^1/$_2$ oz) unsalted butter
220 g (1^3/$_4$ cups) plain (all-purpose)
 flour, sifted twice
7 eggs
1 tablespoon caster (superfine)
 sugar

MAKES 500 G (1 LB 2 OZ)

MELT the butter with 375 ml (1^1/$_2$ cups) water in a saucepan, then bring it to a rolling boil. Remove from the heat and add all the flour at once and a pinch of salt. Return to the heat and beat continuously with a wooden spoon to make a smooth shiny paste that comes away from the side of the pan. Cool for a few minutes.

BEAT IN the eggs one at a time, until shiny and smooth—the mixture should drop off the spoon but not be too runny. Beat in the sugar. Store in a pastry bag in the fridge for up to 2 days.

Sift in the flour and stir until the choux dough comes away from the side of the pan.

CRÊPES

250 g (2 cups) plain (all-purpose)
 flour
pinch of salt
1 teaspoon sugar
2 eggs, lightly beaten
410 ml (1^2/$_3$ cups) milk
1 tablespoon melted butter
butter or oil, for frying

MAKES 12 SMALL OR
6 LARGE CRÊPES

SIFT the flour, salt and sugar into a bowl and make a well in the centre. Mix the eggs and milk together with 125 ml (1/2 cup) water and pour slowly into the well, whisking all the time to incorporate the flour until you have a smooth batter. Stir in the melted butter. Cover and refrigerate for 20 minutes.

HEAT a crêpe pan or a deep non-stick frying pan and grease with a little butter or oil. Pour in enough batter to coat the base of the pan in a thin even layer and tip out any excess. Cook over moderate heat for about a minute, or until the crêpe starts to come away from the side of the pan. Turn the crêpe and cook on the other side for 1 minute, or until lightly golden. Stack the crêpes on a plate with pieces of greaseproof paper between them and cover with foil while you cook the rest of the batter.

CHOUX PASTRY

CRÈME PÂTISSIÈRE

6 egg yolks
115 g (1/2 cup) caster (superfine)
  sugar
30 g (1/4 cup) cornflour (cornstarch)
10 g (1/4 oz) plain (all-purpose) flour
560 ml (2 1/4 cups) milk
1 vanilla pod
15 g (1/2 oz) butter

MAKES 500 G (1 LB 2 OZ)

WHISK together the egg yolks and half the sugar until pale and creamy. Sift in the cornflour and flour and mix together well.

PUT the milk, remaining sugar and vanilla pod in a saucepan. Bring just to the boil and then strain over the egg yolk mixture, stirring continuously. Pour back into a clean saucepan and bring to the boil, stirring constantly—it will be lumpy at first but will become smooth as you stir. Boil for 2 minutes, then stir in the butter and leave to cool. Transfer to a bowl, lay plastic wrap on the surface to prevent a skin forming and refrigerate for up to 2 days.

CRÈME PÂTISSIÈRE

CRÈME ANGLAISE

310 ml (1 1/4 cups) milk
1 vanilla pod
2 egg yolks
2 tablespoons caster (superfine)
  sugar

MAKES 310 ML (1 1/4 CUPS)

PUT the milk in a saucepan. Split the vanilla pod in two, scrape out the seeds and add the whole lot to the milk. (This will give small black spots in the custard—if you don't want them, you can leave the vanilla pod whole.) Bring just to the boil. Whisk the egg yolks and sugar until light and fluffy. Strain the milk over the egg mixture, whisking continuously.

POUR the custard back into the saucepan and cook, stirring, until it is thick enough to coat the back of a wooden spoon. Do not let it boil or the custard will split. Strain into a clean bowl, lay plastic wrap on the surface to prevent a skin forming and refrigerate for up to 2 days.

FRANGIPANE

FRANGIPANE

250 g (9 oz) unsalted butter, softened
250 g (2 cups) icing (confectioners')
  sugar
230 g (2 1/4 cups) ground almonds
40 g (1/3 cup) plain (all-purpose)
  flour
5 eggs, lightly beaten

MAKES 800 G (1 LB 12 OZ)

BEAT the butter until very soft. Add the icing sugar, ground almonds and flour and beat well. Add the egg gradually, beating until fully incorporated. Transfer to a clean bowl, cover with plastic wrap and refrigerate for up to 24 hours.

MAYONNAISE

4 egg yolks
1/2 teaspoon white wine vinegar
1 teaspoon lemon juice
500 ml (2 cups) peanut oil

MAKES 500 ML (2 CUPS)

PUT the egg yolks, vinegar and lemon juice in a bowl or food processor and whisk or mix until light and creamy. Add the oil, drop by drop from the tip of a teaspoon, mixing constantly until the mixture begins to thicken, then add the oil in a very thin stream. (If you're using a processor, pour in the oil in a thin stream with the motor running.) Season well.

MAYONNAISE

VINAIGRETTE

1 garlic clove, crushed
1/2 teaspoon Dijon mustard
1 1/2 tablespoons white wine vinegar
80 ml (1/3 cup) olive oil

MAKES 125 ML (1/2 CUP)

MIX TOGETHER the garlic, mustard and vinegar. Add the oil in a thin stream, whisking continuously to form an emulsion. Season with salt and pepper. Store in a screw-top jar in the fridge and shake well before use. You can also add some chopped herbs such as chives or chervil.

VINAIGRETTE

BÉCHAMEL SAUCE

100 g (3 1/2 oz) butter
1 onion, finely chopped
90 g (3/4 cup) plain (all-purpose) flour
1 litre (4 cups) milk
pinch of nutmeg
bouquet garni

MAKES 750 ML (3 CUPS)

MELT the butter in a saucepan, add the onion and cook, stirring, for 3 minutes. Stir in the flour to make a roux and cook, stirring, for 3 minutes over low heat without allowing the roux to brown.

REMOVE from the heat and add the milk gradually, stirring after each addition until smooth. Return to the heat, add the nutmeg and bouquet garni and cook for 5 minutes. Strain through a fine sieve into a clean pan and lay a buttered piece of baking paper on the surface to prevent a skin forming.

BÉCHAMEL SAUCE

VELOUTÉ SAUCE

70 g (2 1/2 oz) butter
80 g (2/3 cup) plain (all-purpose) flour
1 litre (4 cups) hot chicken stock

MAKES 500 ML (2 CUPS)

MELT the butter in a saucepan. Stir in the flour to make a roux and cook, stirring, for 3 minutes over low heat without allowing the roux to brown. Cool to room temperature. Add the hot stock and mix well. Return to the heat and simmer very gently for 10 minutes or until thick. Strain through a fine sieve, cover and refrigerate until needed.

CHÂTEAU MARGAUX is one of Bordeaux's *grands crus classés*, a classification dating back to 1855 when wines from Médoc, Sauternes and one from Graves were classified according to the prices they fetched. The five-tier classification, from *premiers* down to *cinquièmes* (fifth) *crus* (growths), is still used today, with Châteaux Margaux, Haut-Brion, Latour, Lafite-Rothschild and Mouton-Rothschild (elevated to

WINE

FRANCE IS INDISPUTABLY THE CENTRE OF THE WINE WORLD, AND GREAT BORDEAUX, BURGUNDIES AND CHAMPAGNES CONTINUE TO SET THE STANDARDS ALL OTHERS ASPIRE TO.

The French were making wines from indigenous vines before even the Romans arrived. Over the centuries, winemakers have cultivated an incredible number of grape varieties, eventually matching each one up to the right methods of production, the perfect climate and terrain, from the wet North to the cool mountains and the hot Mediterranean. This fact means that today France produces nearly every classic wine in the world.

CLASSIFYING FRENCH WINE

France's *appellation d'origine contrôlée* (AC) is the oldest and most precise wine governing body in the world. The French attach much importance to the notion of *terroir*, that there is a perfect environment in which to grow a wine and that every wine should demonstrate the character of that environment, so the smaller and more pinpointed an *appellation*, the more prestigious it is. Thus, within the broad Bordeaux AC, sub-regions, such as Médoc, and even individual communities within this, such as Pauillac, may gain their own *appellation*. The AC also defines grape varieties, yields and production methods.

Vin délimité de qualité supérieure (VDQS) classifies less distinguished regions standing between AC and *vins de pays* status. *Vins de pays* (country wines) can be great if they have a strong local character. *Vins de table* should be drinkable.

this level in 1973) all *premiers crus*. The fact that the classification remains in use reflects the suitability of the *terroir* for growing Cabernet Sauvignon, especially the mild climate and gravelly soil, and also the efforts of the châteaux to maintain standards. At Château Margaux, the land is still worked by hand and a cooper handcrafts the French oak barrels. The best of their elegant wines can be aged for at least 20 years.

READING FRENCH LABELS

CHÂTEAU a Bordeaux wine estate

CLOS on some Burgundies, meaning a walled vineyard

CRU meaning 'growth', it refers to wine from a single estate

CRU BOURGEOIS an unofficial level of classification just below Bordeaux's *crus classés*

GRAND CRU CLASSÉ/CRU CLASSÉ a Bordeaux classified in 1855 and usually of a very high quality. Also used in other regions to signify their most prestigious wines

CUVÉE a blended wine from different grapes or vineyards

CUVÉE PRESTIGE a special vintage or blend

MILLÉSIMÉ vintage

MIS EN BOUTEILLE AU CHÂTEAU/DOMAINE estate-bottled, rather than a merchant or cooperative blend

NÉGOCIANT-ÉLEVEUR a wine merchant, often an international firm, who buys grapes to blend and age and finished wines

PROPRIÉTAIRE-RÉCOLTANT growers who make their own wine

WINES can be bought from a *marchand de vin* (wine shop), *négociant* (specialized wine merchant) or *en vrac* (unbottled wine sold by the litre at markets). In wine areas you can also buy directly from the vineyards or from a *cave coopérative* (wine cooperative).

GLOSSARY OF FRENCH FOOD AND COOKING

andouillette A sausage made from pork or veal chitterlings or tripe. Andouillettes are usually grilled (broiled) and often served with mustard, potatoes or cabbage. Some have an outer layer of lard that melts as they cook.

bain-marie Literally a 'water bath' for gentle oven-cooking of delicate terrines and desserts. Usually the dish is placed in a roasting tin, which is half-filled with water.

beurre manié A paste made by mixing together butter and flour. Stirred into sauces at the end of cooking to thicken them.

beurre noisette A simple sauce made by cooking butter until it is brown and 'nutty'.

bouquet garni A bundle of herbs used to flavour dishes. Made by tying sprigs of parsley, thyme, celery leaves and a bay leaf in either a piece of muslin or portion of leek.

brown stock Stock made from browned beef or veal bones. As beef and veal stock are usually interchangeable, the term 'brown stock' is used. The best commercial stocks come freshly made in tubs, though stock sold in cartons and catering-quality powdered stock can also be good.

butter Butter is flavoured both by the lactic fermentation of cream and the diet of the cows from whose milk it is made. Butter from Normandy and the Alps is high quality and has a sweet flavour. French butter tends not to be heavily salted, with the amount varying between regions—Isigny butter from Normandy is unsalted, while next door in Brittany, butter from Poitou-Charentes is salted. Both have AOC status. Use either salted or unsalted for savoury dishes, but unsalted in sweet recipes.

capers The pickled flowers of the caper bush. They are available preserved in brine, vinegar or salt and should be rinsed well and squeezed dry before use.

cervelas A long, fat pork sausage, often flavoured with garlic, pistachios or truffles. It is a boiling sausage (*saucisse à cuire*) and should be poached before browning under the grill (broiler). Ordinary pork sausages flavoured with pistachios can be used instead if cervelas are unavailable.

chipolata In Britain, chipolata means any small sausage. In France, however, a chipolata can be as long as an ordinary sausage but is always much thinner. Usually made from pork and pork fat, chipolatas are used as a garnish in French cooking.

clarified butter Made by melting butter so that the fat separates out from the impurities and water. The fat is then either spooned off or the water tipped away and the butter reset. Clarified butter keeps for longer than ordinary butter because all the water has been removed and it can be used for cooking at higher temperatures because it has a higher burning point.

confit From the French word for 'preserve', confit is usually made from goose or duck meat, cooked in its own fat and then preserved in a jar or pot. It is eaten on its own or added to dishes such as cassoulet for extra flavour.

cornichon The French term for a small gherkin. It you can't find cornichons, use cocktail gherkins instead.

court bouillon A flavoured poaching liquid, usually for cooking fish.

couscous Made from very tiny balls of dough, couscous is usually steamed and served like rice with a main meal. Couscous was traditionally made by hand from freshly milled flour and came in different sizes of grain. Now that it is commercially produced, the grains tend to be uniformly quite tiny.

crème de cassis Originating near Dijon in Burgundy, crème de cassis is a blackcurrant liqueur used in desserts and also to flavour the drink kir.

crème fraîche Often used in place of cream in the French kitchen. Lightly fermented, it has a slightly tart taste. Crème fraîche from Isigny has AOC status.

curd cheese A smooth soft cheese made from curds that have not undergone lactic fermentation. Curd cheese is lower in fat than cream cheese but higher in fat than cottage cheese.

Dijon mustard A pale yellow mustard, made from verjuice or white wine and mustard seeds that have been ground to a flour. Originating in Dijon, this style of mustard is now made all over France.

foie gras The enlarged livers of fattened geese or ducks. Regarded as a delicacy, with foie gras from Strasbourg and southwest France both highly regarded.

fromage frais A fresh white cheese with a smooth creamy consistency. There are a number of varieties, many artisan-produced. Fromage blanc is traditionally used in Lyon's *cervelle de canut*. The fat content of fromage frais varies, which may affect its cooking qualities, but generally it makes a good low-fat alternative to cream.

goose fat A soft fat that melts at a low temperature and is used a lot in the cooking of southwest France to give a rich texture to dishes. Available in tins from butchers. Duck fat can be substituted, although it needs to be heated to a higher temperature.

Gruyère A pressed hard cheese with a nutty flavour. French Gruyère is available as *Gruyère de Comté*, which can have large holes, and *Gruyère de Beaufort,* which has virtually no holes. Although French Gruyère does have a different flavour to Swiss, the two are interchangeable in recipes.

haricot beans The general French name for beans, though the term is also used to mean just a kind of small, dried bean. Dried haricot beans come in many different varieties, including cannellini (kidney-shaped beans), flageolet (white or pale green beans) and navy beans (used to make baked beans). When slow-cooked in stews such as cassoulet they become tender. They also break down very well when mashed to give a smooth purée.

julienne To cut a vegetable or citrus rind into short, thin 'julienne' strips. Vegetables used as a garnish are often julienned for decorative purposes and to ensure a quick even cooking.

juniper berries Blackish-purple berries with a resinous flavour. Used in stews and robust game dishes. Use the back of a knife to crush the berries lightly before use to release their flavour.

Madeira A type of fortified wine from the Portuguese island of Madeira. There are a number of different varieties of Madeiras, from sweet (Malmsey or Malvasia and Bual), to medium (Verdelho) and dry (Sercial).

Maroilles A square soft cheese with an orange washed-rind and a strong smell but sweet flavour. As an alternative, you could use other washed-rind varieties, such as Livarot, or a cheese with a white moulded rind, such as Camembert.

Mesclun A salad mix containing young lettuce leaves and herbs such as rocket (arugula), lamb's lettuce, dandelion leaves, basil, chervil and endive. Traditionally found all over the south of France.

mussels Grown commercially around the coast of France on *bouchots* (poles) driven into mud flats or in beds in estuaries, mussels can be eaten raw but are usually cooked in dishes such as *moules marinière*. French mussels have blue-black shells and vary slightly in size and flavour according to the waters in which they are grown. The mussels grown around Boulogne in northern France are of a very high quality.

olive Grown all over the South, the main varieties of French olives include the green pointed Picholines, purple-black Nyons and the small black olives of Nice, used in traditional Niçoise cooking. Fresh green olives are available from the summer and are picked before they start to turn black, while fresh black olives are available from the autumn through winter. Though green and black olives have a different flavour, they can be used interchangeably in recipes.

olive oil Extra-virgin and virgin olive oils are pressed without any heat or chemicals and are best used in simple uncooked dishes and for salads. Pure olive oil can be used for cooking or deep-frying. Olive oil is made in the south of France, and after picking the olives in the autumn, each year's new oil is available in the winter.

orange flower water Produced when the flower of the bitter orange is distilled, it is a delicate flavouring used in dessert recipes.

oyster Two main species of oysters are available in France. *Huîtres plates* are European oysters, or natives. They have a flat round shell and are better in the winter months when they are not spawning. The most famous are the *belons* from Brittany. *Huîtres creuses* are the much more common Portuguese (or Pacific) oysters, with deep, bumpy and flaky shells. Some of the best Portuguese oysters are grown in Marennes. *Fines de claires* are oysters grown in water full of algae, giving them a green colour and a distinct, iodine flavour.

Puy lentils Tiny green lentils from Puy in central France that are AOC graded. Puy lentils do not need to be presoaked and do not break down when cooked. They have a firm texture and go very well with both meat and fish. Traditionally they are cooked and served with a mustard vinaigrette.

saffron The dried dark orange stigmas of a type of crocus flower, which are used to add aroma and flavour to food. Only a few threads are needed for each recipe as they are very pungent (and expensive).

salt cod Brought to Europe as long ago as the fifteenth century, salt cod's popularity in France is a legacy of the religious need to eat fish on Fridays and feast days. Salt cod is cod that has been gutted, salted and dried, and is different from stockfish, which is just dried but not salted. A centre-cut fillet of salt cod tends to be meatier than the thinner tail end, and some varieties are drier than others so the soaking time does vary. Salt cod is also sold as morue or bacalao.

saucisse à cuire A cooking, or specifically boiling, sausage that is usually larger than an ordinary sausage. *Saucisses à cuire* are poached in liquid, either as part of a dish like *choucroute garnie* or just with red wine.

spatchcock (poussin) A baby chicken weighing about 450–500 g (1 lb–1 lb 2 oz). Spatchcocks are often butterflied and grilled (broiled) or stuffed. Usually one spatchcock is served per person, though slightly bigger ones are adequate for two people.

sweetbreads The pancreas and thymus glands of calves or lambs, sweetbreads are white in colour, soft in texture and have an irregular shape. Sweetbreads should be soaked in cold water to remove any blood before they are cooked.

Toulouse sausage A general term for meaty pork grilling (broiling) sausages, usually sold in a coil.

truffles Considered an expensive delicacy, truffles are a type of fungus and have an earthy smell. The black truffles found in France, specifically around Périgord, are often considered the best black truffles in the world. Truffles are best eaten fresh, but can also be bought preserved in jars, and only need to be used in small amounts to flavour dishes.

vanilla extract Made by using alcohol to extract the vanilla flavour from beans and not to be confused with artificial vanilla essence made with synthetic vanillin. Vanilla extract is very strong and should be used sparingly.

INDEX

BIBLIOGRAPHY

Ayto, John. *The Diner's Dictionary Food and Drink from A to Z.* Oxford University Press, 1993.

Behr, Edward. *The Art of Eating*, no. 48.

Bissell, Frances. *Sainsbury's Book of Food.* Websters International Publishers, 1989.

Christian, Glynn. *Edible France: a Traveler's Guide.* Interlink Books, 1997.

Caroline Conran, Terence Conran and Simon Hopkinson. *The Conran Cookbook.* Conran Octopus, 1997.

Davidson, Alan. *The Oxford Companion to Food.* Oxford University Press, 1999.

Dominé, André, and Ditter, Michael. *Culinaria.* Könemann, 1995.

Dominé, André. *Culinaria France.* Könemann, 1999.

Editors of Time-Life Books. *Classic French Cooking.* Time-Life Books Inc, 1978.

Editors of Time-Life Books. *The Cooking of Provincial France.* Time-Life Books Inc, 1972.

Editors of Time-Life Books. *The Good Cook: Wine.* Time-Life Books B.V., 1982.

Grigson, Jane. *Charcuterie and French Pork Cookery.* Penguin Books, 1970.

Johnston, Mireille. *Complete French Cookery Course.* BBC Books, 1994.

Kazuko Masui and Tomoko Yamada. *French Cheeses.* Dorling Kindersley, 1996.

Millon, Marc and Kim. *The Food Lover's Companion to France.* Macmillan Travel, 1996.

Sinclair, Charles. *International Dictionary of Food and Cooking.* Peter Collin Publishing Ltd, 1998.

Stobart, Tom. *The Cook's Encyclopaedia.* Grub Street, 1998.

Wells, Patricia. *The Food Lover's Guide to Paris.* Methuen London Ltd, 1984.

THE FOOD OF FRANCE

This edition published by Bay Books, an imprint of Murdoch Books Pty Limited
First published 2001.

ISBN 978 0 68102 586 8

Food Editor: Lulu Grimes
Design Concept and Art Direction: Marylouise Brammer
Designer: Susanne Geppert
Editors: Jane Price, Justine Harding
Photographer: Chris L. Jones
Stylist: Mary Harris
Stylist's Assistant: Ben Masters
Additional Photography: Howard Shooter
Additional Recipes: Ruth Armstrong, Michelle Earl, Barbara Lowery, Dimitra Stais, Jody Vassallo, Richard Young, Sophia Young
Map: Russell Bryant
Production: Monika Paratore

Publisher: Kay Scarlett
Chief Executive: Juliet Rogers

Printed by Hang Tai Printing Company Limited. PRINTED IN CHINA.
This edition printed in 2008.

Murdoch Books Australia Pty Limited
Pier 8/9, 23 Hickson Road, Millers Point NSW 2000
Phone: + 61 (0) 2 8220 2000 Fax: + 61 (0) 2 8220 2558
www.murdochbooks.com.au

Murdoch Books UK Limited
Erico House, 6th Floor, 93–99 Upper Richmond Road
Putney, London SW15 2TG
Phone: + 44 (0) 20 8785 5995 Fax: + 44 (0) 20 8785 5985
www.murdochbooks.co.uk

IMPORTANT: Those who might be at risk from the effects of salmonella food poisoning (the elderly, pregnant women, young children and those suffering from immune deficiency diseases) should consult their GP with any concerns about eating raw eggs.

ACKNOWLEDGMENTS

The Publisher wishes to thank the following for their help in making this book possible: Cour des Loges, Lyon; Gérard Ravet, Cour des Loges, Lyon; Danièle Monterrat, Lyon; Michaël Leete, Boulangerie du Pont, Lyon; Jean Perroux, Lyon; Alain Duclot, Lyon; L'Hotel les Ateliers de l'Image, St-Rémy-de-Provence; David and Nitockrees Carpita, Mas de Cornud, St-Rémy-de-Provence; Gerard Driget, St-Rémy-de-Provence; Denis Censi, Fromagerie Du Mistral, St-Rémy-de-Provence; Josette Erard, St-Rémy-de-Provence; Paul Bergese, St-Rémy-de-Provence; Joël Durand, Joël Durand Chocolatier, St-Rémy-de-Provence; Pierre Lilamand, St-Rémy-de-Provence; Van Beeck, Le Petit Duc Patissiers, St-Rémy-de-Provence; Andre Rousson, St-Rémy-de-Provence; Michel Nunes, Aix-en-Provence; Sofitel Marseille Vieux-Port, Marseille; M. Fromion, Marseille; M. et Mme. Delfino, Marseille; M.-J Pichot, Mme. Bizard, Chateau Margaux; Monique Bodin, Christophe Conge, Château Lafite Rothschild; Bristol Hôtel, Périgueux; Gérard Joly, Marchal & Pautet, Périgueux; Jean Paul Armaud, Pondaurat; François Rames, Carves; Angèlique Denoix, St Mayme de Peyrerol; M. Barriere, St Laurent la Vallee; Eric Settbon, St Martin de Riberac; Marc et Marcelle Boureau, Castels; Hotel de l'Université, Paris; Philippe Foulatiere, Hediard, Paris; Marie-Anne Cantin, Paris; Stéphane Nachba, Gérard Mulot, Paris; Corinne Rosa, Paris; Claude et Catherine Ceccaldi, Paris; Vincent Rové, La Sablaise, Paris; Dominique Fenouil, Le Repaire de Bacchus, Paris; M. Jean Luc Poujounan, Poujauran, Paris; Jean Paul Gardil, Paris; Mon Martin Boulangerie, Paris; Sébastien Lay, U.C.L. Isigny-Sainte-Mère, Isigny-Sur-Mer; M. Claude Taittinger, Michèle Barbier, Champagne Taittinger, Reims; Kalinka, Sydney; Camargue, Sydney; Mosaique, Sydney; Brian Allen Antiques, Sydney; McLeod Antiques, Sydney; Peppergreen, Sydney. Rod Johnson and Kayell Photographic; Nicole Lawless and Kodak; Kylie Goodwin, Qantas; Simon Johnson, Sydney; Sara Schwartz, Tasting Places, London; Mosaique Imports; Corso de Fiori; Will Studd; Max Pesch, Ilve Australia.